TWO CENTS

FOR

AFRICA

Beatrice Fri Bime

MIRACLAIRE PUBLISHING
Kansas City / Yaounde

MIRACLAIRE PUBLISHING LLC
Kansas City, (MO) USA

8400 East 92 Terrace,
Kansas City, MO 64138, USA

Email: info@miraclairepublishing.com
Website: www.miraclairepublishing.com

P.O. Box 8616 Yaounde 14,
Yaounde, Cameroon

ISBN-13: 978-0615727370
ISBN-10: 0615727379

Disclaimer
Miraclaire Publishing makes every effort to ensure the accuracy of all the information ("Content") in its publications. However, Miraclaire and its agents and licensors make no representations or warranties whatsoever as to the accuracy, completeness, or suitability for any purpose of the Content and disclaim all such representations and warranties, whether express or implied to the maximum extent permitted by law. Any views expressed in this publication are the views of the author and are not necessarily the views of Miraclaire.

DEDICATION

For my children:

Kerman Kifon Bime, Chiawa Litika Bime, Kindzeka Akere Bime, Chelsea Anje Mbaku, Sandrine Tantoh, and Mary Sevidzem for understanding my lapses in maternal care as I worked on this. I love you always.
Jenabo Abu, Yvonne Njoka, Sebastian Mbaku, Anye, Carlet, Marie, Njang and my other children, for believing in me.

ACKNOWLEDGMENTS

The genesis of this book dates back to the 2004 workshop in Ghana where all the national coordinators and partners for the ILO-IPEC-WACAP project met to work on a manual for STCP farmer field school to fight against child labour in the cocoa commercial agriculture sector.

The book is not meant to be a specialized book on any subject, religion, history or any other. Thus, any errors on those subjects are specifically mine. Many people inspired and encouraged me in the writing of the book.

Special thanks go to the following people:

- Mr. Georges Ntumba, CTA WACAP at the time for the genesis of the idea.
- Dr. Kingsley Moghalu for sharing his world views with me
- Father Tantoh for allowing me to use his sermon
- Prof. John Ngundam for allowing me to tease him on technical education
- My Editors: Dr. David Toh Kusi whose expertise and critical suggestions pushed me to complete the work, Patrick Tata and team (PATAMAE research and editing consultancy – PREC) for their incredible diligence
- Elizabeth M. Mofor for providing the chair I sat on to work

My publishers, family members and friends, thank you.

PREFACE

Two Cents for Africa takes the position that the development of Sub Saharan Africa is the responsibility of Africa as no one can come from outside and develop Africa because there are no free lunches.

Africa, fifty years after independence, has certainly moved forward in many areas relevant to development: Education, Agriculture, infrastructure etc. However, the pace of development for people who just need to copy and paste is slow and at the rate we are going we will not catch up nor close the gap. Without political will and a commitment to develop, Sub-Saharan Africa can't and won't develop.

To achieve even half of its potential, Africa needs a mental revolution, a revolution of people who do not only follow but think. Africa needs to go back to the drawing board, revisit some historical facts and use them to design its path to development. Africans have to understand that Africa is too fragmented to develop. Therefore, we need to come together and strengthen our ties with one another by looking at what we have in common, keeping aside our differences. Together we have to decolonize our mentalities and break the yoke which still ties us to our colonial past. We must become truly independent in a globalized world.

If Africa does not understand that there are no friends in a globalized world since there are no free lunches; if Africa opens its arms and doors foolishly to these new "friends" coming to help propel it towards development then one day we'll wake up and someone would have the title deed to our continent, which may just have cost him two cents.

The Author proposes a stronger African Union (AU) which is the supreme Landlord of Africa and which can be financed through resource extraction fees, providing it the independence to carry out activities to help propel Africa in development. An African Union which will supervise elections and be able to mete out sanctions to countries which deserve to be sanctioned; an African Union which is truly what the founding fathers fought for and intended to put in place; an African Union that will cause *Africa Day* to be celebrated throughout Africa; a celebration of who we are and who we want the world to recognize us to be, strong and united, with regional bodies; an Africa strong and standing up to be counted as well as respected by its peers.

"Never doubt that a small group of thoughtful citizens can change the world. Indeed, it is the only thing that ever has." Margaret Mead

Beatrice Fri Bime

FOREWORD

The propositions made by Two Cents for Africa are solid and unquestionable in their applicability. What Beatrice Fri Bime ultimately adheres to is Africa's development and that the solution to Africa's predicament may be based on education, agriculture, roads and programmed infrastructure or on democratic leadership with a sense of fairness that prioritizes health over military.

Yet the onus according to Fri Bime is on the African in general who must decide to be a producer and not just a consumer so as to generate wealth, meanwhile the taxation systems should be made simple and equitable, and public income and spending made meaningful and accountable to the tax payer.

The reader will particularly enjoy the author's sense of verisimilitude on issues that continue to cause Africa's fragmentation. Therefore, waiting for salvation from without in the guise of aid or favours is detrimental to personal growth. Rather, equitable trade using understood and accepted parameters should be the way forward. However, one big help in the development of the continent has to be unity, and also the expansion of the intra-continental business. One step up of this is a redrawing of the fragmented continental map. The propositions are not for some vague future but now in the hope that the continent of Africa may catch up to the developed and fast growing economies.

Perhaps most significantly, Fri Bime is not defeatist in her arguments in Two Cents for Africa. To her, the only way for the Diaspora and the brain drain syndrome to bail Africa out is a return home and a collective rebuilding.

Fri Bime's Two Cents for Africa is a sustained tenor of passionate discourse on the way out for Africa from divergent perspectives. Therefore, individual readers of this work should take the plight of Africa in hand and work for its emergence. Governments too should set up commissions to study and implement the various components of the package if Africa hopes to move forward. This according to the Author can only be done through a strong African Union.

This Book is a must read for anyone genuinely interested in Africa's development.

Christopher Che
CEO Che International Group, LLC
Member President Obama's Council on Jobs and
Competitiveness

CONTENTS

CHAPTER 1
AFRICA THE BOTTOM BILLION

"The Whiteman and the Blackman started the journey on the same day, but the Whiteman has been to the moon and back while the Blackman is still trekking to the village" Dr **Ali Mazrui**.

Most countries in Sub-Saharan Africa are at the very bottom of the "Bottom Billion"[1] according to Paul Collier. The countries are diseased burdened, conflict ravaged, underdeveloped, under-represented, hunger-stricken and plagued by numerous catastrophes and other disasters you can imagine. However, 50 years after independence many African countries have achieved a lot although much more still needs to be done just to catch up with the world of the twentieth century before that of the twenty first century. We cannot do a thing about the past, but we can decide where we are at now, where we want to be in the future, how we go forward and what we need to get there. At over 50, Africa needs to make up its mind to stand up and be counted or continue to sleep and be overlooked.

If we step back half a century in the 60s right after independence, Africa was sending aid to Korea, fifty years after, Africa is receiving cars and other electronics from Korea and is still waiting to make its first electronics. Does Africa want to develop? It is time to sit down and rethink our

---

[1] The Bottom Billion by Paul Collier

priorities. Where are we right now? Where do we want to be in the next 10, 20, 25, 30 and 50 years? How do we want to get there? We know all the analysis, we understand all the answers, we just need to implement and decide that enough is enough and we can accelerate Africa's development.

Africa needs a revolution beginning with a change of mentalities. Revolution of any type has been at the centre of development in Europe and America and all the developed countries. None would be developed today if they had not had a revolution of one type or another. France had its famous historical revolution; Great Britain had the industrial revolution while America had its war of independence through the Boston Tea Party; Korea, Japan and China have their revolutionary tales to tell. Africa absolutely needs one. Africa needs to wake up, to drink deep and be drunk with a sense of purpose, a vision and mission.

Africa Defies the Rules

What Africa needs is not war or famine but a revolution of the mind: a group of an intellectual mindset that "Thinks", a revolution of the mind starting with a change of mentalities and attitudes; Africans truly proud to be Africans; Africans who have a world view and think of the common good above personal interest. It hurts to see the Whiteman treating Africans as if the colour of their brain is the same as the colour of their skin. But could there be some grain of truth to that?

Sometimes it looks as if Africans (or most of us) stop using their brains when a charismatic or autocratic leader shows up. His word becomes law and everyone else does things to please, praise or cheer him/her. The clouds blowing over Africa seems to have some sleeping drugs in them and one wants to shout "wake up, Africa!" Why should the richest natural resource continent in the whole world be the poorest? Nothing explains why fifty years after independence most failing states are in Africa. Nothing justifies the fact that Africans are disease ridden and disease burdened. Nothing explains why after diagnosing what the African problems are and how to solve them Africa is doing nothing to solve them but is expecting the feeble attempts of others from outside to do the fixes, like some drug addict.

Nothing explains why Africa is happy to just get by, despite the fact that God created it to excel. Nothing justifies why the African past only half matters while its colonial past is still very much present. Africa needs a revolution. Most continents would gladly change places with Africa if they were given the opportunity to do so. Africa has been endowed by God with the best of everything, the weather, its rich soil, forest, natural resources and its place on the world stage. One would think that because of all these advantages, Africa should have been the most developed continent in the world; instead it is the poorest of the poor. Explanations as to why Africa is where it is have defied the most brilliant of minds. Africa even defies the natural law of economics which according to Fred E. Foldvary include:

1. The law of demand: When the price of a good falls, the quantity demanded does not fall. Usually, the quantity demanded rises with a fall in price. Strictly, the law of demand applies to the substitution of cheaper goods for more expensive goods due to a relative change in price. The law of demand also applies to the whole economy: when the whole price level falls, with the amount of money remaining constant, a greater amount of goods will be purchased. (Africa has natural resources which other continents want but hardly ever does any price determination. Rather it allows the market to do that, sometimes to its detriment. A good example is the fluctuation of cocoa prices in the world market).

2. The law of supply: When the price of a good rises, the quantity produced does not fall. Usually, a higher price for a produced good result in a greater quantity produced. (Most African countries sell oil in the futures market at low prices, so when the price increases there

is no effect of that increase on the economy and its people. There is also no incentive for increase in supply in other cash crops like cocoa and coffee because there is no foreseeable gain in increasing production).

3. Law of supply and demand: In a free market, the equilibrium price of a good is that at which the quantity supplied equals the quantity demanded. (If that were so Africa would not sign ninety-nine-year oil leases nor condone price fixing and the future market).

4. The law of unintended consequences: Human actions, and especially governmental acts, have consequences which were not intended and not anticipated by the actors. (Many examples abound of consequences of measures which some government officials took without realizing the long-term effects of their actions on the country and its people).

5. The law of iterated expectations: One cannot use the limited information at some previous time to forecast error one would make if one had better information later (For example, most of the treaties and agreements African countries entered into with their colonial masters benefit only the colonial masters. This is especially true of Africa's mining industry and forest exploitation. The African partners themselves do not know the expected value and prices for the natural resources).

6. Wagner's law: As an economy grows, government spending increases by a greater proportion. (In most countries, government is one of the biggest consumers of goods and services, but the citizens can only benefit from such growth and spending if the government pays its bills or has a mechanism for reconciling its accounts with the private sector).

7. Say's law of markets: The supply of goods will pay the factors of production such that the payments are equal to the value of the product, and therefore aggregate

quantity supplied equals aggregate quantity demanded. (This would be true and benefit the economy if Africa transformed its raw products before exporting them).

8. Law of time preference: People tend to prefer to obtain goods sooner rather than later, and will pay a premium (i.e. interest) to shift buying from the future to the present (Most of Africa's oil is sold in a futures market whether the price changes or not).

9. Law of the market: Statements made by market participants are assumed to be truthful, and products are presumed to be safe and effective unless stated otherwise. (This, as in the case of Africa's natural resources, can only be effective if both parties have the same or equal knowledge of the product and the market; not the kind of blind trust that Africa has exhibited in the past and continues to exhibit).

10. Law of cost: All costs are opportunity costs, the true cost being what is given up to get something. (The opportunity cost of most of Africa's products cannot be truly quantified because Africa walks blind).

11. Law of comparative advantage: Trade takes place because parties specialize in the products which have a lower opportunity cost, rather than merely a lower physical cost. (Africa has historically traded because it has something which others wanted, not because it specialized in anything it had a comparative advantage over).

12. The law of capital goods: Investment in capital goods and human capital expand until the expected return on investment, adjusted for risk, equals that of the long-term real interest rate. (Africa has not yet defined its course, so it is difficult to say that its investment in capital goods and human capital will expand until the expected return on investment).

13. The law of economizing: People tend to economize, maximizing gains for a given cost, and minimizing

costs for a given gain. (The African is still fixed on the now and short-term goals; so long term benefits do not come into play).

14. The Gaffney effect: The public collection of rent equalizes the discount rate for land usage, since otherwise people would have different credit costs for purchasing land.

Africa has land, rich natural resources, money and technology in abundance and can import what it lacks. So what really is pulling back Africa's development? Why is Africa actively aiding its regression? Theories on this issue have advanced points like leadership which translates into bad governance, corruption, laziness, the unwillingness to develop, dependency, etc. But, which country does not have some corruption or any of the other ills? Who can cast the first stone? So what does Africa need? The pointed answer is that, Africa needs a change of attitude and a mental revolution.

It is easy to think that when you give a person lemon and water they can mix them and make lemonade. Well, in Africa you would be wrong to think so. Even if you give Africans all the ingredients in the right measures and ask or show them how to mix them up and make lemonade, they will still not be able because they cannot keep all the ingredients together without losing some on the way. So whatever is concocted you can be sure it would not be lemonade. Is this a very strong indictment of Africa? Well maybe, but even at that the indictment is not strong enough. Does that sound like Africans are stupid or lazy? Not really. They are too intelligent and hardworking for such attributes to hold in the strict sense. If they were lazy, they would not have been kidnapped and taken to foreign countries to build those countries under very harsh and inhuman conditions. Some people say the African has only physical strength. If that were true too, the number of inventions attributed to Africans in the Whiteman's country would not have happened.

Nailah Ellis Timberlake in 2010 compiled a list of major inventions attributed to African Americans including some of the world's most popular inventions reaching back to 1820, when Thomas Jennings, believed to be the first African-American inventor to receive a patent, created a more efficient dry cleaning process. Many years later, Judy W. Reed became the first African-American female inventor with her hand-operated dough kneader and roller. Reed, who was illiterate, signed the patent with an "X".

Other inventors include:

- Laserphaco Probe, Year patented 1986. Patricia E. Bath, M.D., (1942–), first woman to chair an ophthalmology residency programme in the United States
- Oil-dripping cup for trains, Year patented: 1872 Elijah McCoy (1844–1929)
- Shoelasting Machine, Year patented: 1883 Jan Ernst Matzeliger (1852–1889)
- Gas mask, Year patented: 1912 Garrett Morgan (1877–1963)
- Train-to-station communication system, Year patented: 1887 Granville T. Woods (1856–1910)"

With all that the African continent has to offer, it would be a paradise if others took it over. The climate is the best in the world. The continent is conducive to live in all year round. Although some countries have winter, the climate is never too cold or too hot for human comfort.

The natural resources are the highest in the world. It has water, oil, coal, forests, gold, silver, copper, uranium, iron ore and phosphate and many precious minerals. Yet, African countries did not feature on the US and Global equity investor list for 2012, not because they are not rich but because the continent's wealth is dispersed and the countries are fragmented.

What does Africa lack or need to develop? Africa needs a revolution; not a military or another industrial revolution but a revolution of the mind. Africa needs Africans who believe in Africa, love it and want it to thrive. We need an Africa that will once again be a world leader and that can stand up and be counted. "Once again", because if anthropologists have discovered that civilization first started in Africa, then it stands to reason that Africa was once upon a time more developed than the other continents!

Walking through the snow-filled streets of Geneva, covered in layers of warm clothing which are unable to protect one from the minus 10 degree cold, one is forced to think that the Whiteman had to develop by force. How would Africans have coped with long winters? They would all have died or forced to cope and maybe, that is what Africa needs to develop; Force to cope! In this case, it needs a thinking hat and the use of its brains not its hearts only or greedy eyes either.

In the absence of long winters, the salient prods to growth devolve on Education, Road infrastructure, Democratization and Leadership in general. These are the nexal collage of the next rather expanded chapter.

CHAPTER 2
PRODS TO GROWTH

When I was young, I trekked four miles daily to and from school to attend the only Catholic school which was available. Age or birth certificates were not used because none existed; instead, a child's hand had to reach his/her opposite ear before he or she was admitted into primary school. That meant that a short child or one with stunted growth was not allowed to start school early. During my mother's time, she had to go to Bafut or Kom (villages in the North West region of Cameroon), two or three days of trekking. So, any child who wanted to go to school had to live with relatives or live alone to go to school. Today there are state owned, private and missionary schools a few hundred meters apart in most towns and some villages. There are secondary schools everywhere, especially in towns and no child who wants and whose parents can afford their education needs to stay at home. Everyone in Cameroon, as in most African countries, has the opportunity of being educated. The problem is what kind of education are we providing to our progeny? Most educational systems here are still on curricula left behind by colonial masters with few marketable skills being taught.

However, for investors to do business in African at a cheaper cost and propel development as in Asia, the skills, technical knowhow and a favourable environment should be available. The problem is not that there is illiteracy in Africa but that we still have to train Africans with relevant marketable skills which can serve not only Africa alone but the world at large. We need more poly-techniques and technical schools, and fewer schools graduating thousands of students in non-marketable and non-productive knowledge. For a continent wishing to develop, there should not only be a balance between the social and technological studies; there should be more of technology.

My youngest son attends one of the best secondary schools in Anglophone Cameroon and the competition to get in is stiff because they only select the best of the best. After being in the school for a year, he told me he wanted to leave the school before he wrote his GCE ordinary levels. Surprised I asked him why and he responded that he wanted a school with more sports infrastructure. "Fine," I answered "where do we find such a school in the country?" "I don't know" he replied "but there must be". Well the truth is that there isn't.

In the mid-fifties when there were fewer schools in Cameroon, the few offered everything from sports, agriculture, music, and theatre arts to everything else a child needed to succeed in life in various fields. The missionaries and the Whiteman left and gradually these were removed, everything in the curricula that was not "academic" was pulled out. Even religious knowledge was removed.

Are our children being offered a well-rounded education? Can a child leave primary school today and, apart from being able to read and write, grow vegetables in a garden, and sew a button on a shirt or a dress? Children leave schools these days (while in reality those are the schools that make the backbone of any developed nation) without the knowledge of how to boil an egg or even water. How are those children prepared for life? Worse still, many children complete primary school unable to read or write! Yet in times past someone who ended studies in standard three or four could read and write more beautifully than some secondary school children nowadays.

In the 1960s when Sacred Heart College Mankon was established, it took most students a week or more to reach the campus because they had to trek from far off villages without roads and there was no quick means of transport. The college was established to make it easier for those from the grass fields who had had to make the two weeks trek from Bamenda to Buea to study in SASSE College. Due to uncertainty and hazards on the way, older relatives had to travel with these young men to see them safely to school where they would stay for four years or more without returning home because of the difficulties involved. They went to school, happy simply to have made it into schools and worked hard. They built the schools through hard work and sweat, cultivated the vegetables they could eat and some students paid the stipend the missionaries were asking for in kind.

When I wrote my primary school Common Entrance exams into secondary school, commercial and technical schools were not considered because only the old and the dullest pupils went to such schools. So when my deposit to the high standard prestigious secondary school was late by 2 days and I was asked to go to one of the commercial schools in which I eventually ended up, I refused to go to school and told my grandmother that my mother who could read and write wanted me to go to a junk school and that I would rather farm with my grandmother than go to that school. A lot of effort is needed to alter mentalities in educational matters.

My fee was late not because the money was not available. It was available in Buea and the means to send it to Bamenda was only by postal mandate which took anywhere between two weeks and a month to get to Bamenda. Telephones were rare and only found in some government offices while transportation was difficult and roads not very accessible too. Today, I could walk around with any number of phones if I liked and use them to transfer money anywhere. In Yaoundé where I live, I have a Magic Jack number, which is an American number, and it lets me call America and

Canada for next to nothing. That is how much technology has advanced in 30 years. Africa as a continent can choose to advance with the rest of the world or it can sit and wait for advancement to meet it in its backyard. However, even that takes effort and initiative.

Most African countries have been independent for over fifty years. Since then the focus on getting Africa and Africans out of poverty into development has largely been through education. Knowing how to read and write seemed to be the agreed strategy. Adult education was introduced, stayed in vogue for a while and fizzled out. Then education for all by the year 2000 became the universal objective. In the year 2012 that stated objective is still to be met. Truly, there are more Africans educated today than there were before independence. Many more know how to read and write. However, the problem is that instead of education propelling Africa into development and alleviating poverty, education has only created a new kind of poverty. This manifests through the many university graduates who roam our cities without employment looking like they have not had any education at all. Is it education for its own sake or for a practical purpose?

If our educational systems are not goal oriented, directed towards meeting needs and objectives, how can they play a key role in development and poverty alleviation on the African continent? As explained earlier, Africa happens to be the continent with most natural resources, the best weather, and the best of everything God created. Is there any reason why most countries on the continent remain primarily consumer societies? To get the best prices for natural resources, these resources need to be exported either as finished or semi-finished goods.[2] How does Africa make it to

---

[2] It must be noted that the prices for primary products are usually very low while those of finished products (from the developed countries) are usually very high.

that point? Years after all the talk about finished products was discussed on the African scene, Africa still exports products in their primary states, for the developed countries to transform to finished products and sell them back to Africa at exorbitant prices. Developed countries make more from African products, than Africans dream of making if Africa decides to maintain the status quo.

My answer to the call for the African Development Bank's 40th anniversary celebrations in 2004 on how to enhance Africa's educational systems in order to propel the continent towards development still seems valid.

For a General Revision of Educational Policies so that some Provisions can be Geared towards Specialised Education Directed at the Production and Marketing of our Cash Crops and Natural Resources

1. Provide directed education to our young through the establishment or revitalization of schools geared towards our cash crops and natural resources.
2. This approach will create employment, which will consequently lead to an increase in the income of farmers cultivating cash crops.

Increase national income through the transformation of our natural resources and thus GNP. This will create added value, leading to higher prices and ultimately higher returns.

Major Outputs and Activities

	Output	Activities
1	Increased numbers of persons trained in directed education	- enrolling these persons into specialized pilot centres providing on-going training through exchange programmes and linkages with higher education institutions within and outside the country

2	Increased per capita income for local farmers	- employing locals to work in the transformation plants and marketing services - encouraging co-operatives to buy from local farmers - encouraging farmers to join co-operatives for the sales of their produce -encouraging farmers to join savings and loan schemes
3	Increase in effectiveness/ efficiency of co-operatives	- hold capacity-building seminars for members of co-operatives and individuals
4	Increased Gross National Product	- exporting finished products to regional countries, and developed countries

The following strategies should be put in place in order to achieve the needed marketable skills.

Conduct an analysis of all the cash crops and natural resources of a given country. Take any country, Cameroon for example. In preparing our educational policies, the first question to ask is "What are our cash crops and natural resources?"

Identify these cash crops and natural resources like Cocoa, Coffee, Tea, Banana, Rubber, Timber, Oil, Gas, Fish and Shrimps, Mining-gold, diamonds, or iron. The next question is - how do we generate more income from these raw materials by partially or fully transforming them before exporting? The answer would certainly be to find the ability to transform these resources ourselves without relying on our buyers. How do we achieve this?

Establish specialized secondary schools geared towards the cultivation, harvesting, preservation, transformation and marketing of the finished product. How do we make sure that the production of our cash crops is sustained while taking into considerations the issues of environment, gender and quality of the product at the same time?

My proposal is to take any of our cash crops, for example, Cocoa. Go to the cocoa producing area and establish schools in that area which will teach the young people the basics of how to grow such crops and manage their natural resources in an environmentally sound manner. The school should, for example, focus on the planting, nurturing, harvesting, preservation, packaging and marketing of this crop. This will include teaching all the developmental skills of growing a high quality product to enhance better yields without depleting the soil, thus sustaining bio-diversity. This school should have an elaborate curriculum to meet this objective and graduating students may work in their trained fields or enrol into the specialized "higher school". For reasons of economies of scale, these specialized schools can be regional and shared amongst many countries having the same kind of natural resources.

Establish a specialized "higher school" geared towards the extraction, transformation and marketing of the finished or semi-finished product. In order to identify our natural resources, our citizens should be trained on how to identify, extract and transform our minerals and precious stones into finished products before selling them to consumers. That way we have an accurate idea of what we actually have in order to get the best prices for these minerals and precious stones to generate foreign capital. This money will go a long way to help pay for other goods and services needed to develop our countries and would create jobs and improve the standard of living of our citizens.

The proposed strategy for this project is as follows:

a. Identify an existing institution in the chosen community
The proposal is to carry out a survey of the community where a cash crop like cocoa is produced. Identify

an institution like a co-operative, which already deals with farmers and buyers; identify those members of the co-operatives (especially the youth) who need to be trained. Then identify those people who use the resources amongst the members of the co-operative.

b. Develop exchange programmes with international schools

In Cameroon, for example, there are many unemployed agricultural engineers. The most proficient of these engineers should be offered the opportunity to give a home-based training to the cocoa-farmers and youths. Within the course of this training, some of the agricultural engineers can go for further training, depending on the needs of the "higher school", and the most immediate needs of the cocoa-farmers. On return, the engineers will impart their new-found knowledge in the most practical form (i.e. teaching farmers how to use modern technology). This idea is better and practical rather than encourage the current practice where the few Engineers we have seat in offices rather than go out and make use of their expertise. The agricultural engineers would play a key role in starting up the transformation plants and subsequent marketing of the natural resources and finished products, respectively.

With time, the locally trained cocoa-farmers will also go for specialized training, specifically geared towards improving their knowledge of managing their agricultural activities.

c. Set up a pilot school in the product community

After some people have been trained in the processes of transformation, packaging and marketing of the finished product, a pilot school should be set up with the aid of development agencies where the aforementioned processes can be carried out, and the finished product exported to other countries.

The development agencies can provide the start-up capital and buy all the machinery, which is needed for the whole process (from cultivation to marketing of the product). The loan is given to the co-operative, which will buy its members' products at competitive prices, transform the crops and market the finished products. Then from the sales of the finished products, the co-operative will repay their loan to the development agency or Bank. The advantage of giving the loan to the co-operative and allowing the co-operative to be the implementing agency is that it provides community ownership and guarantees sustainability and accountability.

d. Train technicians in the maintenance of the equipment
The machinery used in the process of transforming the cocoa into chocolates and other products derived from cocoa are expensive. It would not be enough to buy the machines. Some sections of the school or university to which the project has been linked would have to provide on-going training in the maintenance of this equipment in order to ensure continuous production.

e. Collaboration with local universities and technical institutions
In addition to initiating exchange programmes with schools outside the country, efforts should also be made to collaborate with local universities situated in areas where cash crops such as coffee and cocoa are cultivated. The co-operative, together with the university and the development agency should prepare a curriculum for the pilot school. For the maintenance component of the project, the pilot school could also collaborate with existing technical institutions such as the Polytechnics.

f. Lobbying
Given the projected success of this approach, it is envisioned that after the success of the pilot programme, other

co-operatives and local communities can take initiatives to influence the decision making process by lobbying government to replicate the process in another community and also make this a national education policy. This way we can guarantee government policy changes, commitment and continuous implementation of the approach. Government policy will also guarantee sustainability and provide some measure of surety to the lending development agency.

g. Evaluation

The pilot school concerned with the education of our youths in terms of our cash crops and natural resources should be tested in two communities with the same crop over a five-year period. After that, it should be evaluated in terms of the number of jobs created, the standard of living of the community, the way the loan is repaid, etc. Following this, the system should be replicated in the country for all other cash crops and natural resources. It is at this point that it could be replicated in other countries. It is inevitable that a project of this nature will most certainly lead to development and poverty alleviation in the country in particular and on the continent as a whole.

Sustainability

This project will be sustained through community participation and ownership. The co-operative is a permanent structure of the community that will manage the resources at its disposal, continue the education and training of members of the community to transform, preserve, and market the cash crop grown in the community. Children and young people are the most sustainable resources, which any country possesses. Involving them in this project inevitably provides sustainability.

The Role of Development Agencies
The role of development agencies will be to:

1. Provide funding for the preliminary training at a higher institution outside the country
2. Provide funding for the training in the pilot schools
3. Provide funding for the purchase of the machinery and equipment
4. Supervise and monitor the project
5. Replicate the project for other cash crops and natural resources
6. Replicate the project in other countries

The Role of the Government
1. Create an enabling environment in its national Universities to test the pilot project
2. Revise national policies to enhance some part of its national education towards the country's cash crops and natural resources
3. Replicate the success of the project on its own
4. Guarantee the development agencies' loan

Features that Make this Approach Different
The proposals contained in this project are aimed at development and curbing of poverty through education, focusing on our educational strategies in favour of our cash crops and natural resources. This approach requires that we start with what we have, see how we can make more out of it by transforming the crop ourselves before marketing it rather than exporting raw materials which are transformed and then sold again to us at exorbitant prices.

By such a focused and directed educational approach, we ensure that jobs are created in our countries and we become a producing community rather than simply a consumer society. Sustainability is assured through community participation and ownership through institutions like the co-operative. The standard of living is increased along with national income.

Replicability

The proposal is very practical. It makes use of existing structures, taking into account the immediate needs of the community. The project can be successful in an environment where the Government is flexible enough to let the private sector (especially agriculture) innovate new methods of reorganizing the sector, while allowing for limited government intervention.

The only changes that need to be made in the proposal in exporting it elsewhere are the identification of the cash crops and natural resources. The approach attacks poverty in a practical way while reaching the rural as well as urban areas. Development naturally comes to the country after this approach is implemented. This proposal has been made with the intention of contributing to the economic development and social progress of African countries by focusing some of our educational policies towards the abundant natural resources and cash crops our continent is so blessed with. The concept comes from the idea of most African countries who have been saying for years that we as a continent collectively and as individual nations will gain more from our cash crops by transforming them into finished products or partially finished products before selling them. After diagnosing the problem, steps have not been taken to ensure with the provision of the capacity for the necessary transformation.

When structures for transformation exist, there are owned and run by foreigners with little or no technological transfer to the locals. In Cameroon, which is the third cocoa producing country in Africa, the sole structure which transforms cocoa is French.

This proposal attempts to bridge that gap in our educational systems by gearing the education of our next generation towards practical vocations, which takes into consideration our export crops and natural resources. It is hoped that if implemented, the proposal will help to create employment, generate income for its target community, increase National Income and standard of living, and propel development towards the millennium goals.

Sample community college or technical school: Because the other economies are not going to be sitting there stagnant while waiting for Africa to play catch up which at the current rate is impossible, the only way for Africa to close the development gap is to go through Education which can accelerate development. This has to be appropriate education connected to the perceived strengths of the continent, education centred on the continent but with a worldview.

Agriculture is only a sample. For as earlier said, there has to be a balance between general and specialized education. For example, after the advanced levels where general education is done, some community colleges can be put in place to train and perfect students with the following skills:

a. Construction:
The main issues of this sector are represented in the numbers and quality of trained technicians. The numbers of building technicians coming out of training are currently low. In addition, the quality leaves a lot to be desired. This shortcoming is manifested in the quality of building finishing in all aspects:
- Construction standards may not be understood. It is questionable if there are any national standards on this particular point. If they exist, do technicians actually understand these standards or know how to read them? These same comments can equally be addressed to the design, construction and certification aspects of building construction.
- Auxiliary services such as electrical wiring, plumbing and others such as landscaping are very poorly done. In the electrical wiring angle, there are evident risks of fire in a very high percentage of the buildings because

cables are laid without any consideration for such risks and without taking into account standards required.

The above shortcomings suggest that training institutions themselves provide poorly designed programmes of training on the one hand, and the quality of teaching staff might be questionable on the other hand.

Programmes of training for both training of trainers and trainees have not changed with technological advances, even in the civil engineering and housing sectors.

b. Basic Needs

Using Cameroon as an example, Cameroon is divided into five so-called Ecological zones. Although most technical services required in the different zones are the same, each is somehow different and may require specific training for the industries and commerce in them for the future. As an example, training of technicians in building construction and its auxiliary services, automotive technologies etc. require the same training. For buildings, an additional dimension needs to be added to take into consideration local conditions and available technologies such as cooling approaches to offices and homes.

In general, specific industries should be planned for the regions based on the natural resources located in the zones. In the same token, institutions of training should contain programmes that include those found in all other zones as well as those programmes specific to local industries.

It must be stressed that if Cameroon must be seen as an emerging economy by 2035, training must be modernized so that goods and services destined for a competitive global market place must meet quality and productivity demands.

At the bottom line, African youths need to be taught all the things which industries need in order to function effectively and this should be sector specific. Other African Countries can emulate Angola a small African country already emerging. They are training their people on everything concerning diamonds in order to add value before selling to reap bigger profits. It is currently the country with the highest growth rate according to World Bank statistics.

c. Build Centres of Excellence

These centres of excellence should be able to help Africa develop and add value to all of its natural resources before marketing them. The minimum requirements for these centres should be the equivalence of the GCE Advanced level because these centres are meant to go beyond understanding the existing techniques. These centres should encourage research and scientific publications too and that may just be where the time machine for slimming will be made.

Agriculture

When I was young the farming cycle for maize and other food crops was once a tedious year, from clearing to tilling, to planting, weeding and harvesting. Due to ingenuity or necessity, maize and other crops can now be cultivated all year round. The cash crops used to be coffee and cocoa, very labour intensive and had a long time for any return on investment. Today, maize, beans and other short-term products have become cash crops. In spite of these gains, famine and hunger affects 38 Million people in Africa yearly while, every day, almost 16,000 children die from hunger-related causes. That is about one child every five seconds. The World food programme estimates that 12 million children have been orphaned due to hunger and malnutrition. Furthermore, "The World Food Programme estimates that 22 of the 30 high-risk countries in need of external food assistance are in Sub-Saharan Africa". How then may the agricultural sector in Africa be developed?

Agriculture in most African countries has remained in the hands of subsistence farmers with no access to farm to market roads and consequently transportation and market remains a nightmare. A typical farmer works all year round and it is heart rending to view the amount of waste and losses. A floor full of cocoyam harvested and transported home rots. The same eyesore occurs with most other crops and tubers.

A cooperative to store and market these items would be a great economic booster. A cooperative could move such items to cities and business centres for sale and save the losses and waste. The result would be an increase in standards of living all round even for city-dwelling non-farmers who would have to send less financial assistance to their rural relatives.

My agricultural proposal to the African Development Bank in 2004 was that, although small holder farms must remain, the sector needs to be organized. It is a known fact that Cooperatives have worked in developed countries and should work in Africa.

Small farmers can be encouraged to group themselves into cooperatives according to crop-types, or according to regions, sectors or even neighbourhoods. All cotton farmers can take their cotton or the cotton can be picked at the farm, weighed, processed, sold and the farmers paid according to the quantity and quality of the cotton they gave, with the cooperative holding a small fee for running cost and price guarantees.

In Cameroon, cooperatives were encouraged by colonial masters and the cooperatives thrived. There were cooperatives for coffee, cocoa, cotton and other cash crops. The members managed these cooperatives themselves and succeeded, but once the colonial masters left and government brought people who had no stakes in the products to manage the supervising boards for these cooperatives, embezzlement and stealing brought the structures to the ground and that discouraged many farmers from cultivating these cash crops and their land was diversified to other crops.

In most African countries transformation and preservation is a foreign word. As much as we produce individually or collectively, when crisis come we are unable to sail through it. For a continent with one of the richest soil deposits, it is unimaginable that more is not done to preserve and or transform food crops. The sheer waste and spoilage of farm crops in Africa is estimated by the World Bank, the World Food programme and other actors to be as much as 80 percent. It is mind-staggering to imagine attainment of a 90 percent usage rate; the magnitude wealth from more proper preservation alone would reverse the plight and economic status of Africa.

Africa has to make a conscious decision to no longer want or need food aid and to work hard to use what God has freely given it; others have to use, reuse and toil with manure, fertilizers and other chemicals. This way they produce more than enough to eat and even to export. Importing food is not only wrong but also sad for most African countries because their trade balance is in deficit. Africans, both individually and collectively, need to work to reverse the situation and one of the ways in which to do so is by working together according to their comparative advantages, specializing in what can best be produced and producing such in huge quantities and high qualities to sell to one another.

Infrastructure

It is not news to anyone that traveling in Africa is both difficult and hazardous. It costs more in terms of time and money to travel within Africa than traveling in some cases from Africa to Europe and vice versa. From Abidjan one has to take a plane to Paris before going to Chad. That not only makes it long, tiring and time consuming but more expensive. From Yaoundé to Bamenda it takes six hours on roads with some parts which are so bumpy and jarring to the muscles. That is as much time or even more than it takes to reach Paris from Yaoundé by air.

The Germans almost won the Second World War because they could move their heavy equipment from place to place faster than the allies could and this was thanks to their huge road network, a lesson the Americans learned and have implemented in their vast country. Is there any possibility for Africa to develop without being connected to each other? The African Union is ineffective without good communication, roads and train networks linking African countries to each other. OAU talked about a Trans-African road and train network since its inception. This has remained a pipe dream.

Every country needs to have a master plan of all the possible roads that exist and will exist in that country for fifty or more years. In order to promote regional communication, national roads should join those of neighbouring countries. There should never be a case of an area being developed without taking into consideration the national master plan of road network. Infrastructural questions need answers as part of national planning for housing. What are the short, medium, and long term plans for these infrastructure? Will there be tram ways? Trains, electric cars or buses? Why not learn from those who are already using these things and prepare accordingly? Why provoke unnecessary insurrection today which would only make development in the future more expensive and consequently cause unnecessary pain to people when houses and other property would have to be destroyed?

When I look at some of our cities, I feel like we learn nothing from our past errors. The capital of Nigeria was moved from Lagos to Abuja because there was so much chaos in Lagos, almost impossible to fix. Abuja seemed a good answer and is a fantastic place for now. But give Abuja twenty years and one would have to ask what lessons were learnt from the chaos in Lagos. Abuja is already turning into an expensive Lagos with dirt and slums. After that, what next? Is the Capital city once more going to be transferred after twenty years or are they going to have to destroy and build infrastructure that could have been planned for in the first place? Have the planners no growth statistics from which to extrapolate indicators?

To the African Development Bank, whose "primary aim is to contribute to the economic development and social progress of African countries individually and collectively", I dispatched the following paper on its 40th anniversary:

"This paper explores the ways in which road infrastructure directly leads to poverty alleviation and development in a country such as Cameroon. This includes the construction of trans-national, national, and farm-to-market roads, which will not only play a key role in addressing the issues of rural poverty, but will also promote intra-regional trade, specifically within the CEMAC zone. Because of its simplicity, it is foreseeable that this approach can easily be replicated in other African countries.

Introduction

After fifty years of independence, the development gap between Africa and other regions of the world is widening instead of closing. The idea of infrastructure, roads and communication networks is not innovative and the call for new approaches to infrastructure development, specifically with regard to road construction, has not been inventive. Giving loans without *personal contribution,* (if I already had the money then why would I need foreign assistance?):

- participating in the identification of the road network,
- encouraging community participation and ownership in the venture,
- supervising the construction of the road network,

And (in the case of trans-national and national roads), putting in place a team to collect toll from which a sizeable portion of the revenues generated can be used to repay the development agents' loan. Another portion of the revenues will be used to develop other sectors, including the agricultural and health sectors.

The paper also seeks to show that by simply constructing farm-to-market, national, and trans-national road networks, development will directly follow through increased access to education and health facilities, increased standard of living, a

Beatrice Fri Bime

decrease in rural poverty, and an overall decrease in rural-to urban migration. Furthermore, a trans-national road network would also open up export opportunities to major markets, in its promotion of intra-regional trading. The paper states conditions necessary for the success of this approach and how it can be replicated anywhere.

Problem Analysis

The issue of development and poverty alleviation has dominated world focus and strategy for decades now. It seems that the more the world talks about "developing the underdeveloped" and lessening the great disparity between rich and poor nations, the greater the gap between developed and less developed countries (LDCs) widens. In the African continent, for instance, initiatives focused on increased access to health and education facilities have been advanced as methods to reduce the ever-widening gap. In the case of road infrastructure, the idea of constructing key roads that would connect rural farmers to urban markets is often disregarded in favour of national highways that are more frequently used by the public. To the state, this makes economic sense. However, this is in the short run and not so in the long run. Where do the goods that need to be transported on the national highways come from? From the rural areas. Even with laudable efforts to develop Africa, and numerous books and articles on development, 'it is obvious that past keys have not yet unlocked Africa's potential for growth'.[3]

Roads

Development and poverty alleviation cannot succeed without the inclusion of *communication and road networks*.

The first question one asks is what are the features that make a country developed? Roads certainly are one of them.

[3] Dollar, David and William Easterly. *The Search for the Key: Aid, Investment, and Policies in Africa.* Washington, D.C.: World Bank, 1996.

Many will report on the nightmare of travelling from one African country to another on a non-existent road. Not to mention, it is also rather costly (financially and in terms of security) to move from country to country. The negatives outweigh the positives and 'development' may not reach certain remote areas of a country due to general inaccessibility.

It was virtually impossible for one to access the town of *Akwaya* (located in the Southwest Region of the country) without passing through Nigeria. Until 2012, there was no road connecting the rest of Cameroon to Akwaya and the natives did not have any access to urban markets in Cameroon. Had provisions been made for the construction of a road to Akwaya before now, this would have brought development to the area which is still enclaved and backward. The point is that, for an African country like Cameroon to be properly integrated into the world economy in the new millennium, extra efforts should be focused on the development of road networks.

The Givens[4]
a. Job Creation
Engaging in road construction projects reduces the unemployment rate in a country, by providing opportunities for skilled and unskilled workers. Job creation and an elevation in the standard of living for the majority of the people will create social stability in most African countries.

    i. Local contractors to whom the project of building roads will be awarded would in turn employ local workers to carry out general and specialised tasks. Granted that road construction projects are only temporary, and that the workers may not have been equipped with the necessary skills to become self-supporting, efforts

---

[4] These are all the already known and identified advantages of building roads and opening up communication networks across Africa.

should be made to train and equip unskilled workers (employed in road construction and maintenance) with the necessary skills (e.g. welding, vehicle mechanics, small enterprise development, among others) to become self-sufficient, so that when the project is completed, the workers are also empowered to become self-employed.

National and trans-national projects would also reduce rural poverty, as locals will be trained and employed for road maintenance projects. Furthermore, locals will also be employed to man the toll gates, therefore not only generating personal income, but also generating national revenues, some of which may be directed towards debt reduction.

b. Open Communication Networks

Road construction projects connecting rural to urban areas also increase the demand for communication networks, including telephone lines. Communication demystifies the stereotypes about other countries and its citizens, breaks down boundaries, unifies people and changes the traditional concept of 'home.' With access to new information, remote areas of a country can become more 'developed.'

c. Decrease in Rural Poverty

A road construction project can also bring about a decrease in rural poverty in the following ways:

i. Creating more jobs will lead to a better standard of living for the village dweller, and also decrease rural-to-urban migration. This may also have a positive effect on the issue of overcrowding in urban areas.

ii. The problem with agriculture in our countries is that most of it is subsistent agriculture. The farmers cannot live off their efforts because they do not have access to market with the result that, statistically sixty per cent of harvest is lost. The construction of farm to market roads would enable villagers to sell their products at the source, affording to buy their basic needs, increasing their standards of living as well as that of their relatives in town on whom they depended for these basic needs.

iii. With the building of roads, would come hospitals, healthcare centres etc. This will also result in an increase in life expectancy.

The cry of most parents who cannot send their children to school is either poverty or non-availability of schools. Road building would ease building of schools, and encourage Teachers to go to rural schools where they are transferred and with increased income, parents would be able to sponsor their children in school.

Innovative Approach

Since the givens are known and accepted, what problem is there in the building of roads, railways, airports across Africa? The general argument has been that as much as infrastructures will create jobs and alleviate poverty, building and maintaining them is too costly. Many countries in Sub-Saharan Africa cannot afford these costs. This too, is a given.

In the past, when development agencies and other international organisations provided loans for road construction projects, the money ended in foreign banks inaccessible to Africans because of corruption on the part of authorities. We have 'tarred roads' on paper which do not even exist in reality. Consequently, the development agencies decided to verify Government determination by asking these countries to contribute a small percentage to development efforts. However, even these small percentages seemed too much for most countries to afford.

Cameroon for instance does not have enough money to finance a major road construction project, as this would greatly affect the finances of other sectors, including the health sector. Asking the Government of Cameroon to pay a certain percentage for a road construction project may cause the Government to impose immediate hardships on the Cameroonian populace, as the payoffs of this project may be somewhere off in the future, while the pain is immediate.

For a road construction project, this paper proposes that development agencies should finance the whole project, with the understanding that the money the Government would have otherwise used as part of its quota to finance the project, can instead be directed to more pressing matters like health and education.

The inability of a country to make a financial contribution should neither stop nor hinder development and poverty alleviation efforts. Instead, the development agency or organization should bring its money, with governments' co-operation, identify priority roads based on needs, call for bids, supervise the award of these contracts, follow up and supervise the construction of the roads. Following this, they can recuperate their money plus interest through the collection of tolls using a team they will have put in place. After the development agency would have collected its investments plus interest or the return on its investment, the road now remains and is controlled and maintained by the community and state. The trade-off of building roads this way include:

1. **No increase in taxes.** The advantage of development this way is that development and poverty are alleviated without increasing taxes or the burden thereof on the citizens.

2. **Funding agent's role.** The role of the funding agency is much more increased. Their involvement is longer term, personal and vigorous. With the involvement of the funding agents in a longer term, jobs too are created for all categories of people.

3. **Community involvement.** Involving the communities everywhere the roads pass gives them a feeling of ownership, leading them to be protective towards the road. In some communities without cohesion, or an

understanding of the advantages of having roads pass through their area, some sensitisation should be done to raise awareness.

4. **Social services.** The money which a country could have given as personal contribution if they had it can then be put into other priority areas like education and health.

Conditions for Success

For this proposal to succeed, the following conditions have to be met.

1. Government Policy and Co-Operation.

No matter the good will of development and funding agents, this proposal cannot succeed without the express co-operation of the country involved. There must be a signed agreement of the intentions and the success of these initiatives would depend to a large degree on the terms of the contracts, which are signed with governments. In the case of a change of government, there should not be a rescinding of the contract or any terms of the contract anywhere.

2. Existence of A National Road Map

For national roads, there should be an existence of a national road map. For Trans-National roads, there should be clear roads linking one African country to the next. The repairs and maintenance of these Trans-frontier roads should be the collective responsibility of the countries involved and the African Union.

3. Sustainability

The cost of building roads is certainly more expensive than the cost of maintaining them. Therefore, after teaching the community and the country good practices in collecting tolls and maintaining the paved roads, the development agency leaves the government and people to do so on their own.

Replicability

No two countries are the same. However, given the same conditions, and taking into consideration social and cultural differences the proposal can be replicated in other countries beginning with a few pilot countries; these countries should be ready to meet the established conditions (as outlined in the previous section on *Conditions for Success*)

Democracy

After the fall of the Berlin Wall in the 1990s a wind of democracy swept across the world. Africa was not left indifferent. In 20 short years, the gains of democracy have turned into nightmares of dynasties. Children are succeeding their fathers in seeming democracies. All across Africa the wind of dynasties is building up and gathering momentum while the world observes impotently or indifferently? Kabila succeeded his father in the undemocratic republic of Congo and Ali Bongo has done in Gabon (It is only fair to note that in the latter case the heir seems to be a better ruler than his father and Gabon is poised and on the path towards development)

Most developed countries have two at the most three political parties. But on the other hand, most developing or failing states at the bottom of the bottom billion have over a hundred different political parties with as many seemingly different opinions which are not really different. Cameroon in the last count in 2011 had over a hundred political parties, a phenomenon echoed in other African countries.

Recommendations: In spite of the merits of democracy, failing states should not waste so much time and resources on many different parties or on democracy as prescribed by foreigners. African democracy needs to be tailored to fit its own local conditions and circumstances. Before the Whiteman came, Africans had effective management systems based on traditional roles of chieftaincies and royalty different from that of developed countries. The traditional rulers were chosen and groomed from birth, depending on the culture, and women were included in decision-making. The checks and balances within the fondom did the trick.

Belly politics is the current currency. There is nothing new in the syndrome that goes to reinforce the fact that democracy cannot thrive in a country where poverty is chronic. Real democracy is not yet possible in an African continent where the number of people dying of hunger is alarming and where those who are sick and able to afford treatment or care only make democratic intention an abstract notion and nothing more.

From trade Unions to small common initiative groups or *njangi*, through to political parties and even households, it is manifested that when people have power at any level, they are prone not to want to give it up. In this scheme of things, it is hard for heads of states to give up power voluntarily, with all the adulations and everything else that goes with it.

There should be an instrument that is supreme, higher than any individual, party, group of people or head of state. For concrete checks and balances, the constitution should be that instrument which cannot be changed at the whims and caprices of anyone. Constitutional issues have been shuffled like cards in most African countries. For this reason, such countries might as well forget about national sovereignty. If any constitution needs to be revised in order to maintain a Leader in place, then the international community can and should come in and, if need be, use force to get the leader out by reason of insanity.

The Rwandan genocide of 1994 which took the lives of many Tutsis and moderate Hutus is an indictment of our times. It is a result of our collective indifference and sins of omission. It is another indictment of our attitude of looking the other way "when things don't concern us". In a globalized world something which happens in a remote village somewhere in never heard of *Ngolemakong* can affect the man in China or the woman in New York. We had better wake up as a whole and take a closer look at our surroundings and do something about what we see and what we can do before events overtake us. For pointers, it is perhaps relevant to cite an example:

Cameroon, said to be one of the most stable countries in the CEMAC region, is a bomb waiting to explode. Like any bomb, if it is not diffused on time, then whether we like it or not, it will explode someday over issues which could have been taken care of long before they become explosive.

By nature or design Cameroon was separated and ruled by two different colonial masters who left different impacts and attitudes on the people, which unfortunately make the union between the two sectors an uneasy alliance. The Anglophone is naturally proactive while the Francophone is reactive. This does not make for good bedfellows. To make matters worse "La Republique" has opted out of the union by reverting to its pre-reunification name without giving thought or feeling to the former West Cameroon. The "minority" voices in West Cameroon who consider May 20th 1972 and therefore the change of names in 1982 as an overt act of annexation keep rising.

A name is at the heart of an identity and along with the cultural disparities between East and West Cameroon begs the question "What makes a people citizens of a country?" Amongst others is the feel of affiliation with and sense of belonging to the country. The knowledge that the country would defend that individual's right and that, that individual will be willing to fight for and die protecting that country. Above all, the knowledge that one can become anything they can and want to be in that country. How many Cameroonians of Anglophone origin have the audacity of hope to become President of Cameroon?

In Canada where the same configuration exists in reverse, there have been since 1871, 22 Prime Ministers of Francophone Quebec region out of a total of 28, thus only six from the majority Anglophones. In Cameroon, on the other hand, Anglophones at best are treated like poor cousins from some village visiting their rich relations in the city, and at worst they are simply ignored.

Cameroon is the one country where all the same parameters which led to the Rwandan genocide have also been present and the only thing which has so far saved Cameroon from genocide is the over two hundred tribes and ethnic groups in it. Come to think of it, why can't Cameroon be called just Cameroon if it needed a name change? One would be surprised how much a simple thing like that can diffuse the tension that keeps rising from the voices crying that there has been a divorce and a breach of the original contract signed between la Republique du Cameroun and West Cameroon in Foumban. The issues are perhaps not as simple as that and just changing names without a change of attitudes is not enough, but for starts, these could be seen as a show of good faith and hope.

Unfortunately, the absence of such signs of good faith is often read as bad faith. This is one of the thorns that prick the Anglophones to reread history and question the relationship inflicted on them.

As it is, former West Cameroon or Anglophone Cameroon is bigger in land, resources and people than Namibia, Benin, Togo, and Eritrea. They could have been given the third option. Had they been given, would it be at peace or would it have degenerated? Proponents of separation think it would have been much better and it would have developed faster.

Leadership

Most of Africa's woes have been blamed on its leadership. Rightly or wrongly, leadership does have its contribution to the development of Africa just as in other countries and continents.

Leaders who are not hands-on managers are bad enough for the failing states but to have a Leader who is not only ignorant but cares nothing for his country is such a burden that no amount of good intentions from the people and the state, can serve any purpose. Citizenship carries responsibility, even more so leadership demands the same. Leadership is not tyranny but facilitation and productive service.

It is true that at every given moment in history a country gets the leader it deserves. This is a numbing way of explaining the phenomenon of support for a head of state that every objective person sees as a curse to the nation. It is the justification as it were for the terrible fact that adulation is rendered to a head of state who instead of saving the nation they pledged to rule rather pillaged and brought their country, its people and the country two years backwards for every year they have been in power? Compounded by the natural love for power, a President who is lied to by the people surrounding him/her about how well he is running the country and how he is cherished by the people even when they know that election results are all a sham, such a President would not by any stretch of the imagination want to relinquish power.

It is amazing that some autocratic Leaders really believe that they can continue doing the same thing over and over and expect different results. The image conjured is of a woman whose friends tell her how beautiful she is. If she stays around them long enough she can start believing herself the most beautiful woman in the world. If she cares to look around she would see beautiful women everywhere and take her rightful place in the stretch of beauties rather than be deluded by her friends who flatter to please her. The genuine Leader, the good President is one who needs and should seek people who can look them straight in the eye and tell them the truth, no matter how much it hurts; tell it to him in an honest and objective manner. African Leaders should take the challenge to have people like that to advise them. If only for that reason alone, Julius Nyerere would still top the "list of African Leaders we need and should have".

An objection may be raised that virulent critics of a regime become the greatest choir singers when appointed into the ruling government. The explanation is that the appointee goes by the rule of the game, "Scratch my back, I scratch your own" as synthesized into a Cameroonian pidgin slogan.

No leader who is truly working in any case can take the stress of running a country for more than two terms. President Jimmy Carter aged twenty years within four short years, Bill Clinton and Barack Obama all went grey before our eyes. The only reason African Presidents can stay in power or want to do so forever, is that they are not leading; rather they sit to eat, eat and eat while the citizens chafe and chafe and chafe while the economy recesses.

Someone rightly said in one of our forums that, "If citizens have a stake in the success of their country, then they would be less likely to buy into political, economic or financial instability; they would understand better the notion of cohesion, nationality, nation building and a sense of shared purpose and achievement leading to pride in their fatherland". For this to happen, a change in attitudes and behaviours is an absolute necessity. True, a change in attitudes and behaviours is not as simple as it sounds yet it is doable and achievable. For a collective change in attitudes and behaviours, people must be made to find unifying rather than divisive factors. Unifying factors in Africa far exceed the divisive ones. The marvel is that the "divide and rule" policy from Africa's colonial past has worked across all of Africa to these days. Africa needs a revolution of the mind, a revolution that celebrates Africa day in full knowledge of who the African is, where the African comes from and with an open-eyed choice of where to go. This will permanently guarantee emergence from the stagnation and bane that now characterizes it. Mental revolution is a destination guarantee.

Health Care

Health is the most prized possession any government can give its citizens. Without a healthy workforce, how can any nation hope to develop? Yet in the national budget of most African countries, less than ten percent of the budget is spent on health or health personnel or health infrastructure. The whoops of embarrassment came to me recently. A Doctor friend was hit by a car and had severe headache as she was being rushed to the hospital. At the hospital where she was specializing, the x-ray machine was not in working order and it took over six hours for her to be attended to by her colleagues. The X-ray could only be done the next day at another hospital. In another case, the car of a former colleague of mine was hit by a driver who after hitting a pedestrian tried to escape. My former colleague was rushed to a Clinique without emergency services and she bled to dead. These are quick succession events that bring forth the blighted image of the health sector in Cameroon, a situation that any day can be reported all over Africa. Health services lack even basic emergency kits. Chances are that even the decision maker who does not see the need for these services is not exempted from falling victim someday.

More is spent on arms and the military and its personnel earn more for less than one tenth of the education of medical doctors or other highly educated corps. This goes on in most countries to keep the leaders in power, not to protect the country or its citizens but to protect the Leader. Misplaced priorities are an apt description here. In 2001, the AU had an extra-ordinary meeting of heads of states in Abuja to collectively see what to do about the pandemic of HIV and AIDS ravaging their citizens. They agreed to put 15 percent of their national budgets in health. Malaria and tuberculosis were added and with an instant contribution of a hundred thousand dollars from Kofi Annan, the then United Nations Secretary General, the Global Fund to fight against HIV and AIDS, malaria and tuberculosis was born. In spite of foreign aid and contributions, it is obvious from the realities in the field that hardly any of the African countries kept to the Abuja agreement.

According to the KC team:

The Abuja Declaration that was adopted in April 2001 by African leaders declared that the response to HIV/AIDS, TB and other related infections would become the highest priority in their national development plans. Leaders committed themselves to take all necessary measures to ensure that the needed resources were made available from all sources, and that they are efficiently and effectively utilized. This pledge was made to target the allocation of at least 15 per cent of their annual budget to the improvement of the health sector and to mobilize all the human, material and financial resources required to provide care, support and quality treatment to their populations living with HIV,TB and other related infections. Now, 10 years down the road, few countries have achieved this target with the regional average remaining at 7 per cent and even then this is largely influenced by international donor funding not domestic resources.

Failure to keep Africa Healthy

- Not enough on health communication and social services
- AIDS handling has been a big failure as the infection rate keeps rising or just stabilizing in most African countries. What that translates to is that as people are being put on treatment even more people are waiting to start treatment. Programmes have to be integrated. There has to be continuous sensitization and awareness raising on the issue of HIV and AIDs. More efforts need to be put on prevention besides care. What goes on now is that as care and treatment prolong peoples' lives and give a higher standard of living, the resources

to place newly infected persons on treatment dries up and there is also donor fatigue as donor domestic problems take precedence over foreign direct assistance. As in many other sectors, it is time for Africa to take care of its sick.

- Dependency on foreign aid for research and treatment. For a continent which is the most affected by the pandemic, it is amazing that not enough money is put into the research for combating these diseases. There is still high dependence on foreign partners for solutions for these and other African problems.

- A call for an all-fronted attack: Rethink strategy and prevent rather than treat – use everything, cultural, morals, religion, abstinence, fidelity – discourage polygamy and generational relationships. The war Africa needs to be spending on is the one to prevent its citizens from HIV viral infection rather than spending on arms which in most countries rusts from disuse. The war Africa needs to be fighting is the one to feed its starving populations. Africa's war should be to develop and leave its wealth home, in Africa instead of taking it and filling Swiss Banks. The war Africa should be fighting is the war for integration and cohesion and not a war against each other. Africa needs to be looking at what makes it African and how to use the abundance of natural resources which God has given them. Progressive and more successful economies are doing these for themselves. It is time for Africa to go after these healthy practices.

CHAPTER 3
PRODUCTION NOT CONSUMPTION

'I am not a separatist but I was there for the All Anglophone Conference (AAC) one and AAC two which later became SCNC because I believe in justice. To deny, for example, that there is an Anglophone problem in Cameroon is to live like a donkey with its head in the sand, and to let the problem fester and grow out of proportion and be used by some people for selfish interests. Real or not, the perception of a problem does exist. If Cameroonians are equal why is the presidency and other positions out of reach for Anglophones? Fifty years after independence, there has never been an Anglophone Secretary General, no Anglophone Minister of Finance and other positions'

Most governments in African countries are the biggest employers. Thus, civil servants feel their livelihoods threatened rightly or wrongly if they do not belong to or adhere to the principles of the political party in power. Thus, because of the perception of government power and control, civil servants feel obliged to serve the party in power instead of the country. In most cases because they belong to the party in power they feel and act like untouchables.

Upon my return to Cameroon from the United States with an MBA, I reluctantly joined the civil service as a contract worker in order to keep my family together. After a couple of months doing the same boring exercise that anyone with minimum education could do, I was willing to leave. I told my director (an Anglophone who later became Prime Minister) I wanted to move to another ministry and he accepted but when we went to see the Director of General Affairs (A Francophone) who needed to endorse my transfer, he was flabbergasted when I explained that I was leaving because I had no job satisfaction. He could not understand. "You get your salary don't you?" he asked.

The truth is I had not started receiving the salary after four months but I told him the salary did not really matter because I had not gone to school to come back and do some mindless exercise of writing salary advances and switching names and grades. Anyone could do the job. He refused to let me leave promising that there was another service coming which he thought I would have the kind of satisfaction that I was seeking there. However, my mind was made up as I really could not take another day of the routine work. So I took off to the ministry of trade and industrial development where I worked for eleven years and when the economic crisis hit and work slowed, I could not stand going to the office, sitting all day and being paid without producing any results. It was time to move on again. This time I opted to do so through a voluntary departure scheme which was an outlet recommended by the World Bank and sponsored by the French cooperation. In a bid to do structural adjustment in failing states, the IMF and the World Bank recommended slimmer and more efficient and effective civil services. These recommendations were aimed at reducing costs, redeploying public funding and rendering public services relevant and left to the barest minimum. In Cameroon the move was sponsored by the French cooperation through the funding it put at the disposal of the government to pay off those people who were willing to leave especially from none essential positions.

However, many of those who asked to leave towards the end of the exercise including me have never been paid entitlements. The reason is simple. This was an externally driven activity and there was no government commitment or budget to follow through when the external funding ended. The last time I went to the Ministry of Finance, the Chief of Service who had my calculations and who handled the documents told me simply that there was no budget to pay us. Since our payments were calculated, more than seven ministers had passed through the Ministry of Finance and none has been able to find a budget they can use to make the payments. She then asked me why I had stopped my salary. I should have continued taking it until the day I was paid my entitlements. I laughed and asked how I could continue receiving government salary when I was not working for the government and had since moved on. She told me that was the way it was done and I told her all I was interested in were my entitlements nothing else. She looked at me strangely and under her breathe said "these Anglophones." Yet, stealing from the government is not a language issue in Cameroon, but there are some things that Francophones and Anglophones do not understand about each other.

Societies do not and have hardly ever been known to develop through the public service. For development, veering from public service into the private sector is the turn. People working in the public service should be those who have the calling and the desire to serve the people and not to be served. It should be a genuine desire and vocation not a job for the sake of a job. Surprisingly the economic situation of most African countries hardly affords its citizens with the choice to follow their vocations. Therefore, what we have are people working without a passion for what they are doing. This in effect also affects the work ethics of most countries in the continent.

The proposition here is for a strong but small and efficient public service which pays comparable salaries and a vibrant and strong private sector which employs over eighty percent of the work force. For this to happen, the government needs to put in place incentives to enable the private sector to thrive. These incentives could include tax breaks for start-up businesses, capacity building for small and medium sized enterprises, easy access to credit, land, infrastructure, electricity and a sound judiciary to protect people's property so that foreign investors can come in without fear of being exploited or cheated. To quote Abraham Lincoln in this respect, *"Nearly all men can withstand adversity. If you truly want to test a man's character, give him power. Add money to that and you have a dynamic situation"*.

Wealth Creation and Generation

Definition: Wikipedia says "Wealth is the abundance of valuable resources or material possessions." While the United Nations definition of *inclusive wealth* is "a monetary measure which includes the sum of natural, human and physical assets. Natural capital includes land, forests, fossil fuels, and minerals. Human capital is the population's education and skills. Physical (or "manufactured") capital includes such things as machinery, buildings, and infrastructure." and the traditional definition by, Adam Smith, in *The Wealth of Nations*, describes wealth as "the annual produce of the land and labour of the society". This "produce" is, at its simplest, that which satisfies human needs and wants of utility. In popular usage, wealth can be described as an abundance of items of economic value, or the state of controlling or possessing such items, usually in the form of money, real estate and personal property.

In economics, net wealth refers to the value of assets owned minus the value of liabilities owed at a point in time. 'Wealth' refers to some *accumulation* of resources (net asset value), whether abundant or not. 'Richness' refers to an *abundance* of such resources (income or flow). A wealthy individual, community, or nation thus has more accumulated resources (capital) than a poor one. The opposite of wealth is destitution. The opposite of richness is poverty.

Adam Smith was the first to realize that the *Wealth of a Nation* was not in the accumulation of commodities or in the resource reserves that a nation may happen to possess. Rather wealth exists in the productive knowledge of its people. The ability to efficiently transform resources (factor inputs) into desired goods and services represent the true source of a nation's wealth. Adam Smith went on to say; Physical and human capital represents the true embodiment of wealth. This wealth is used to generate factor income as a payment for the production of desired goods and services.

The creation of wealth is based on knowledge - the ability to take raw inputs and convert them into output with value greater than the sum of the individual parts. Additionally, this value is determined by correctly assessing the demand for the output - how it will satisfy needs and wants. The creation of a restaurant, airplane, or apartment building (physical capital) all represent a contribution to a nation's wealth in that they all generate a future stream of income based on the willingness of the members of that nation to purchase food services, transportation services, or housing services to satisfy specific wants.

Economic growth therefore is *the sum* of the rate of growth in technology in addition to a weighted average of the rate of population growth and the rate in which capital accumulates.

These are all good theories and practical things which the African continent can and should embody in order to develop. The easiest way to build wealth is by creating value for others, yet with all the natural resources it has how much value does Africa put on the resources to make others want it? This takes us back to knowledge and Africa's educational systems. The rest of the world had already created most of the new technology yet there are still areas into which African scientist if they exist can venture. With tales of tsunamis, hurricanes and floods constantly, Africans with their black magic knowledge can put their heads together and create as my son said a bomb that will divert storms, hurricanes and floods without killing sea life. It is doable.

In a globalized technologically advanced world, what is the African an expert in? As said before, not even the knowledge of its natural resources does Africa possess. The question therefore is in what areas can the continent, beginning by regional bodies, identify as their niche to develop and specialize? What are the new market demands? Is it exotic foods? Could it be tourism to some ancient place with modern day facilities? What value added can Africa bring to the notion of green revolution? Africa needs to come out of its consumer mode into one of wealth creation. This too can only happen with help from Africa's policy makers and a commitment to see the continent move forward.

Money as a value of wealth

It has been said that "Money is energy and energy is movement". Without movement, there is no way money can multiply and there is no way a country or a people can develop. Thus, development does not depend on the amount of money a country has, the potential to make a lot or how much its leaders have looted but where the money is kept and what is circulating in the country. It is no secret that most money looted from Africa is found in foreign Banks. What happens is it does not only impoverish the country, but because of the multiplier effect, for every dollar that is taken out of the country, the real effect is over ten times the loss of the value of the money to the country and to the citizens. Africa can therefore not develop if fixed in a consumer mode and hand-to-mouth existence. Africa needs to generate wealth within the continent and, most importantly, keep it in the continent.

Adam Smith's definition of wealth in his *The Wealth of Nations*, is an all englobing definition and easy to understand. Africa, which has the greatest natural resources and labour to boot, should be the richest continent in the world by that definition. But no! In development economics, wealth is defined as "anything of value" which other people need. Even at that, Africa would still be rich, because the rest of the world needs what Africa has. However, the problem as already stated before is that Africa itself does not know what it has, nor does it know how to value what it has. In order to get value for what God has blessed her abundantly, Africa needs to add value to its natural givens so other countries will need and value them. First, it must train itself to have value for all its resources. This leads the discourse back to the issue of educational strategies, linking them to national resources.

Data for the following table obtained from UNU-WIDER World Distribution of Household Wealth Report

Table

Region	Percent of world population	Percent of world net worth (PPP)	Percent of world net worth (exchange rates)	Percent of world GDP (PPP)	Percent of world GDP (exchange rates)
North America	5.17	27.1	34.39	23.88	33.67
Central/South America	8.52	6.51	4.34	8.49	6.44
Europe	9.62	26.42	29.19	22.8	32.4
Africa	10.66	1.52	0.54	2.36	1.01
Middle East	9.88	5.07	3.13	5.69	4.1
Asia	52.18	29.4	25.61	31.07	24.1
Other	3.14	3.7	2.56	5.4	3.38

After Asia, Africa has the world's largest population but the world's lowest percentage of GDP. Africa has the natural resources, the population and prospective market.

Added to these, the continent has some of the world's greatest intellectuals. So what is holding it from developing? Africa is so low on all the indexes that it is ashamed to lift up its head and speak with the rest of the world. Yet, that must not be the attitude to take. Africa must decide to stand up and be counted if it hopes to develop.

Taxation

World Bank statistics on starting a business show that most of the countries with difficult conditions such as high taxes and shaky environment are found at the bottom billion. There is certainly a need for taxes to aid development. However, increases in taxes and long start-up time for businesses impede rather than aid development.

From Biblical times, Tax collectors have never been viewed in a positive light. Yet they do work which needs to be done. The reason is simple. It is said that it is difficult to see an honest tax collector. Taxes keep being increased and businesses have a low survival rate in countries at the bottom billion because the taxes which should go into the public coffers end up in private pockets while the government coffers receive little of its expected budget. Tax collectors go out and threaten business people into bribing instead of paying taxes because most business people are ignorant of what taxes to pay in what percentages.

In Cameroon, the rules have been simplified and business people just need to go close to taxation centres and depots to learn how to calculate their taxes and what kind of taxes they need to pay. Information is priceless. For the business person to visit any centre, he/she has to be aware of the existence of the centre and the services it provides. Given that most informal sector business persons are not necessarily literate, the information and training needs to be contextualized and given in a format everyone can understand. Even if someone cannot read or write, he/she can count in their language and he/she can also calculate the taxes in the same way rather than are fooled by unscrupulous taxation agents to offer them bribes instead of paying honestly into the public coffers.

Perhaps the best way to collect taxes is indeed to simplify the process so that anyone who can and wants to do business gets an idea of what is required without strain. Taxes should be paid into the government treasury and nowhere else. Governments in turn should be transparent in telling their citizens how much comes in from which sources and how the money is spent. In the late seventies, a whole family was butchered in their home in Douala and there was only one accidental survivor who was a baby. Allegations had it that this was done to silence the guy because he had talked about oil money in Cameroon.

Today nothing has changed because oil resources in most African countries are still the biggest state secrets. One wonders what would happen if the revenues from oil and how the money is spent were made public.

The opportunities

The theme "The time is now" for the 2010 world cup for football played in Africa for the very first time in its history was not a mistake. This is Africa's time and opportunity to be developed. Africa is still virgin land with many opportunities in most sectors. The search for the new world has come and gone, but for most African countries, nothing has changed so there is a lot to be done and can be done. As the second largest population in the world, Africa is a potential market and producer. If the right systems were put in place, labour would like for the Asians, be cheap. Yet it is hard to conceive of this happening without infrastructure for electricity, water, road, transportation and the necessary skills.

Talking about skills, when the world cup goes to a country or continent, there is guaranteed growth in every sector. But when it happened in South Africa, the most developed country in Sub-Saharan Africa, most of what FIFA paid the country was redeployed out of the country because there were hardly sufficient skilled workers to build the stadia for the games.

Archaeological findings have found evidence to show that Africa is the cradle of civilization. On the premise that life is a cycle, if Africa is the cradle of creation then the world will not end without civilization coming back to Africa. Given the cyclical nature of history then, civilization is bound to come back to Africa to complete the cycle. That time is now. That notwithstanding, Africans can decide to come together and build the continent in varied ways:

Track public income and spending

America, the most developed and arguably the richest country, in the world, publishes and everyone knows how much its chief of Staff earns. No matter how much money the US President made before coming to office, the President's annual salary is $400,000 which is actually less than most CEOs make. Few African countries can guess what their heads of states earn. Tracking public income and expenditure is like looking for the proverbial needle in a hay-sack. The salaries of most of the Presidents of SSA countries in the bottom billion is the biggest kept secret which then gives them the right to use government funds as if it were their personal or private farm.

The other no-go area is that of oil revenue. In most of the oil rich Sub-Saharan African countries, with the gap between the actual revenue and what is put into the government treasury or reported widening as the greed of the leader increases. The poor, miserable mocked with the endowment of titular citizenship, without even the right to their own shadow, watch on mutely because when it comes to state resources it is a matter for a select few. Yet, if more people would just read, they would find extensive evidence from different sources of how much revenue the country is making and then be able to calculate exactly how much is being pilfered to and kept in Swiss accounts and how much is being mismanaged and wasted.

While in Geneva, each time I went on mission to one African country, except Tunisia, I wondered when and how Africa was ever going to close the gap between it and the developed economies. Back in Cameroon celebrating 50 years of independence, evidence of progress did show, some strides towards development. But these strides were not long enough nor in the right directions. As pointed out earlier, in the education section, in spite of an increase in education on the continent in general, there is an acute lack of skills in most relevant areas, from nurses to doctors to technicians etc. While the doctor-patient ratio (an index of the number of Doctors available per 1,000 or 100 patients) in developed countries ranges between 170 to 500, the ratio in Africa ranges between 151 to 2 with Tunisia and Seychelles topping the list at 134 and 151 respectively with Malawi coming in at the bottom with 2 according to Africapedia.

Transparency and Accountability

African countries need transparency not only in government spending but also most especially in government revenue. Where is the money coming from? Where is it going to? Is it being judiciously used? In a one income home, the non-working spouse would not be angry if he/she knows how much the other spouse makes and how the money is being spent. What area of the country is contributing most to the national cake? Is the area being developed in accordance with its contributions to the national cake? If not is the mechanism for distributing the national income seen or perceived as being fair? If not, can the state and people do something about it?

A reading of Dambisa Moyos' *Dead Aid* reveals the contrary but perhaps Africa does need Aid; Africa needs focused direct aid which actually gets to the intended recipient, without most of it getting lost in administrative procedures. The curse is in just how rich SSA countries are and how much is being pilfered. From this perspective, indeed aid should stop. Pushed to the wall, Africa with no other choice would have to develop: forced to develop or choose to die. The people will rise up and will not only be forced to think but to act. Pushed to the wall, mental revolution will turn Africa round and push her where the only option would be development.

Before a harsh judgment on Africa is passed for the billions of dollars that have been poured on her with nothing to show for it, the reality should be zoomed on. How much of the so-called aid has actually reached Africa? How much is spent on Administrative costs and technical capacity building by expatriates from the donor countries because Africa 'lacks' the capacity to manage the aid? Who is really benefiting from the aid? Is aid something that donors put in place in order to create jobs for its citizens or is it really to help propel Africa towards development? Is aid just a measure put in place for politicians to clear their consciences because they have to be seen as doing something to help the needy? If Africa is fifty or over fifty years old now, is it not time it took the reins and run its own countries according to different capabilities and capacities? The Chinese have it that it is better to teach a man to fish so that he can feed everyday than to give him fish only once. How many of these aid programmes have transferred knowledge and expertise? Africa needs to go back to the drawing board with its donors and take a closer look at what is actually happening in the aid world.

African strength

Some Africans work hard. They are successful Africans who have succeeded through determination and sheer hard work. Very few African billionaires inherited their wealth. However, some successful Africans fear to go to their villages because when they do tales of black magic and death are heard.

The problem is that without knowing or considering the route these people have trodden, there are jealous friends or relatives lurking around to harm them instead of celebrating their successes with them. If many of the stories one hears about witchcraft in Africa are true then the conclusion is that Africa has some knowledge which could lead it to development if they could harness it.

Before the Whiteman came to Africa, Africa was able to heal its sick through traditional medicine. Africa's traditional medicine was more specialized than what the Whiteman brought or what is called traditional medicine, is today. There were people who could treat only children (paediatricians), those who could treat only women (gynaecologist) and those who treated specific illnesses for the different sexes. They also did not ask exorbitant fees like are being charged today. It was not the panache of one person who can treat everything that currently exists nor was there rampant destruction and poisoning that is the current norm.

The African has incredible strength. But it is strength not to progress, but to do harm, to destroy and to kill each other. The African can send thunder to kill, frighten or act as a warning to a debtor. The African can hold rain for days on end. The African can concoct poisons to kill his/her fellow man but not an antidote for the poison. The African can make himself disappear and fly in the night using sardine tins made by the Whiteman, but the African is still trekking to the village while the Whiteman has been to the moon and back many times. If the African could harness all the paranormal powers positively he would not only have been to the moon and back but would have invented many weapons of mass destructions to sell to the rest of the world and why not become a super, super power. But so long as African strength remains in individual hands to harm rather than do good, Africa will never develop according to the standards of the rest of the world.

Barack Obama and his African connection

Before Barack Obama came on the scene I, like most women was rooting for Hilary Clinton to win the democratic nomination and become the first female American President. I cannot begin to say here all the reasons why I like Hilary Clinton. Besides her intelligence, I was seating in our living room in Arusha, Tanzania with my husband and watching her husband's swearing in and commented on the inappropriate way she was dressed, exactly two minutes before the journalist did too. By then my husband was already saying what insignificant things women take into consideration. When the journalist went further to comment that the Ivy League graduate could care less about what she was wearing, my admiration for her went up instead and I followed her and her husband's Presidency very keenly.

Barack Obama for me at first was just another black man like Jesse Jackson who will make a lot of good speeches that will lead no way. But the more I followed the American campaign and listened to the contestants, Barack Obama won me over not because he was black but simply because he had everything it took. From confusion between him and Hilary, I was won over and I became more American than an American. I bought anything that had to do with Barack Obama and his wife Michelle who balled me over the day I saw her climb onto the rostrum in a skirt that was slit on the side. My GOD! I shouted in my apartment in Geneva, that sure is one chick with a presence.

The more I read and heard about the Obama's the more I loved them. But I said one thing. If I were Obama, I would be the hardest American President on Africa. African roots or not, it is time that someone forced Africans to stand up and take responsibility for themselves.

I was up all night the day of the elections in the US until I knew for certain that Barack Obama had won before I dosed off for a few minutes on my sofa to wake up and go to work. I cannot explain it. I took the same shortcut to the tram stop every day for over two and a half years in Geneva and probably met the same people on that short cut daily. However, the morning after Obama won the elections I grew five inches taller and had such a smile on my face that everyone I met greeted me with a smile that morning. I may never meet the Obama's but being an African in a European city, I shared his victory with him and just for maybe a short while my status changed.

The day Obama was sworn in, I had some Magistrate friends from home and some others in Geneva. I cooked, chilled three or four bottles of Champaign and we sat in my tiny apartment, ate and as soon as Obama took the oath of office, we popped the Champaign as if we were right there in Washington sharing the moment with the rest of the world. The next morning, as I walked to the bus stop again, there were still many more congratulations. I am not Kenyan, I am not American, but by being black, Obama's victory was part of every black person's victory and mine. Like me many African countries and Africans celebrated that victory. Some Africans even expected some changes in favour of Africa from the Obama administration.

They forgot that even if Obama has some African roots, his first allegiance is to America and to Americans. The one thing which Obama's presidency should teach other countries and Africans especially is that in a free and fair society hard work pays. People look at how slim and pretty the Obama's look. They forget the hard work they put into being the way they are. They get up to exercise when I and most people are snoring in bed. They have studied hard all their lives, attended the best schools and succeeded through hard work. People should never forget the lesson that to get anything requires hard work and perseverance. The general run of Africans have lost all value of patience, and want to have something for nothing, to have everything without working for it, everything easy and cheap without struggling or making any effort and then expects to develop. Barack Obama did not get up one morning and decide to become the President of the United States, and like, magic succeeded. He planned and strategized for it for years. He campaigned all over the US. He worked hard and his hard work paid off.

From the Presidency of Barack Obama, Africans should take this home that anything is possible with GOD and hard work. Africans should learn something positive from his Presidency rather than sit and hope that because he is there, America should increase its Foreign Direct Assistance to African countries. For the reason that he is there, the FDA to Africa from the United States of America should reduce and eventually stop. Maybe, just maybe, that will push Africans to the wall and with their backs to the wall, they will have no choice but to sit up, think and work to be the best they should. The election of President Barack Obama then can be seen by Africans as both a challenge and an opportunity for Africa and Africans all over the world. If Obama wants to help Africa he should be the hardest American President on Africa so that Africa can stand up and be counted.

As the first African American President, he is a source of pride and affirmation for the African and Africa. As an African American, Obama has proved to the world that people of African descent are neither animals nor stupid; the challenge now for other people of African descent is to follow Obama's example and work very hard for the continent to rise and be counted.

CHAPTER 4

TALENTS, ETHICS, AND BAD GOVERNANCE IN SSA COUNTRIES

God created every human being a unique individual with different gifts and talents. The way we use those gifts or talents will depend on our socialization process. Therefore, every member of a society is useful and can make a contribution to the development and welfare of that society or continent in which they are found. There is a general belief that most Africans have talents for sports not academics, yet there are very few sports schools in the continent.

Ethics are rules that govern an individual as prescribed by the society they belong. In Africa, it does not matter which country an individual comes from, the continent is seen as endemic to corruption due to bad governance which leads to the cycle of poverty that is also endemic to the continent.

As said before there are many Africans educated now than at independence, but how many of these Africans are using their knowledge for the good or development of their continent? How many are using their talents to enhance prosperity on the continent? From football players, Medical Doctors, Nurses and other skilled professions the African is found outside his/her continent rather than within.

Diaspora

I don't know about other countries but there are thousands of Cameroonians out of the country who have been receiving salaries for years while they are not in the country because of a porous civil service which is centralized. If one calculates that each of them was being paid just 100,000 francs a month times 10,000 people it will come up to 1,000,000,000 a month, twelve billion a year times the number of years they are out. They render their services to their host countries and milk their home countries dry. The least and first thing for them to do is to stop their salaries and return what they have stolen. The consequences of having ghost workers are an inflated budget and increased unemployment because others cannot be employed to replace them. Some continue receiving their salaries while they are abroad until they are ripe for retirement and then they return and make retirement documents and continue to receive where they had not sown. They are the first to come and do census when census are going on. They stay outside and criticize a government they are helping to cripple. They should return home and help to build their country. And yet the question whether the diaspora can help to build a country is hard to answer. It is like driving a remote controlled car. There is no real control. On the other hand, they can come and render their expertise and their services to their countries in order to help propel Africa towards development. So diaspora assistance really means home coming.

Brain Drain

Africa is not developing not for want of talent or intellectuals. The continent is so full of exported intellectuals it cannot afford not because it does not appreciate them. Foreign countries that can pay higher salaries lure them. Brain drain is a great cost to Africa and it is better for Africans to return home and serve their countries in any capacity. However, until Africa can provide a conducive, competitive and enabling environment for those outside, this will not happen. The many African Doctors working in Europe and America is a clear example of another kind of slavery. In most hospitals at night and over the weekend in developed countries, Africans take up those shifts which are not proper for "white people" to work.

Some African medical staff spend the whole weekend at work, and sure, they earn double for their efforts and send some of the money home to their parents and siblings. Yet that is not the actual cost of the brain drain to African countries. The true cost of the brain drain is the fact that before most Africans leave for the West, they have had at least the GCE advanced level, their fees paid for by their parents. Some parents even borrow to send these children out, at a lot of personal sacrifice that is never taken into consideration when brain drain is calculated. The fact that the African goes out to study and remains there to work means that the developed country is actually using labour which has been paid for by an underdeveloped country. That cost is enormous. Besides, these Africans go out and take on foreign manners and forget being African, a thing perhaps more costly to the continent than any financial remuneration can ever be properly calculated or compensated.

The real cost of brain drain as stated in most international statistics needs to be revisited and Africa needs to make more efforts to keep its children home or bring them back. Since Ghana started its upward spiral the number of Ghanaians who have returned home and are prospering is an indication to other African countries of what can happen when they make the effort to keep its children. Which truly African child would want to trade all the sunshine in Africa for the cold winters if they can have only half of what they get out there and if they can feel that they can work or do anything when and if they want to? Certainly not many would choose the Whiteman's country instead of Africa.

Donors

Donors come in with their conditionality's dangling carrots in front of the noses of hungry and desperate people and of course these countries make commitments to donors promising to carry out reforms and adhere to some policies and as soon as the aid is given the commitment is forgotten. It is strange that most donors continue to give the aid even when the commitments are not kept. Are the concepts of aid and globalization all just a game of interest, where the donor or developed country says "I will, if you" and the developing country replies "okay, I have, please" and the donor gives his aid and when he realizes that the developing country hasn't, he says "but you promised that …" while the developing country replies "I did not lie, I was only …" and the aid changes hands and the games go on each protecting their interest while the interest of the beneficiary is not sufficiently addressed.

Thus, instead of helping countries to move towards development, donors have turned a blind eye on the realities on the ground, and are fuelling corruption and maintaining the status quo through autocratic regimes in power. The arguments rightly or wrongly are that when aid is stopped, the intended recipients would suffer because the leaders will still take the little that the country produces and leave people with nothing. Maybe that is exactly the reason why aid should be stopped so that people can get off their backs and think and be forced to do something about their situations.

The joke in Cameroon is that because there is so much food to eat and beer to drink, not many people care who or how the country is being run. This is a statement of a fundamental fact of Cameroon as a consumer society as nothing is preserved because eating is done at harvest. Nothing is transformed; nothing is stored for later use.

A closer look at donor organizations shows that what they give with one hand they take with the other. Are they just creating jobs for their citizens or they are truly sending aid to develop the underdeveloped world? Is anyone truly interested in developing Africa or everyone is interested in being present so that they can continue to exploit Africa? Africans need to analyse this closely and decide what to do and who to trust.

Yet the African leadership profits from the situation and certainly would not bite the hand that gives them heavenly comfort.

I was a national consultant for evaluating a project that took place in the North West region of Cameroon. The Donor had given over a million dollars for the project. However, less than 15 percent of this entire budget reached the beneficiaries. The rest of the money was spent on Administrative costs, vehicles and running around fees. I saw how happy the beneficiaries were for just the little that actually got to them and I wondered how much improved their lives would have been if 75 percent of the funding had actually reached them and how much more sustainable would the project have been.

Donor Responsibilities

We need proud Africans, Africans with respect. Yet no one ever bought respect. Respect has to be earned. The only way to earn respect in the political arena is not to be a beggar, not to be in need or needy. Donors have a responsibility if they truly want to get the bottom billion out of the pit and close the huge gap between the have and the have not's. They need to be able to look policy makers in their faces in their own countries and the recipients' country and with all due respect politely tell them the way they see things exactly as they are.

The economy of South Africa depends on less than 1% of their GDP on FDA (Foreign Direct Assistance). So, no donor can come in and ride rough shod over them and tell them what they should do or how to do it. And know what? Because South Africa is an emerging SSA country which does not need and hasn't shown to the world that it's desperate, every donor clamours to go there so that they can write their success stories from there. Often a so-called "good will" people who have left their countries to come and work in a developing country look down on these people. Where is the African's pride when its Ministers go to meetings without preparation, and allow themselves to be talked down by some wet nose white boy young enough to be his son, just because he represents some Donor? No one brings the air Africa breathes, nor the continent and natural resources which already belong to Africans.

Development Agencies

The mission of most development agencies is to help the underdeveloped to develop while at the same time meeting the objectives of their countries or the United Nations. The objectives are always very noble and praise worthy. However, the question remains, after so many years of development aid and activities what sustainable results are there to show for the presence of these organizations?

In most cases, with all the good intentions and willingness to help, even after identifying what is wrong and what needs to be done, the agencies lack the courage to tell sovereign governments the truth as they see it. What most will say in private in very intimate circles is so different from what they will say in public. Why do people and agencies need to play games when the lives of millions could be changed if only someone stood up and spoke the truth as they saw it?

If one listens even to Ambassadors who are leaving a country after serving there for a few years, they always say that the country is on the right path even if they do not believe it themselves, and then a few years down the road, give them another opportunity, and their analyses are different.

Africans do not only need a mental revolution but Africans who are vocal and Leaders who are patriotic and committed. Countries like Ghana, Rwanda and Angola will become truly emerging economies within the next decade and it is thanks to nothing more than good and visionary Leaders. A few pockets of successes will show up but it will neither be enough to spill over to the other African countries nor will it be enough to get them out of the bottom billion, but the good news is that they are headed in the right direction.

Donor Harmonization or Country Harmonization?

For years, people have talked about donor harmonization for the maximization of output efficiency and the curbing of some of the waste that have been and that are currently going on in the aid and development agenda. However, donor harmonization is difficult because of self-interest and different donor requirements and formalities.

So, if African countries were not too needy they would not accept nor go through all the complications that they have to go through from some donors. Billions of dollars have trickled, into Africa in the last fifty years but there is nothing to show for it. While corruption, bad governance and deviation of the funds have had their toll, the failure also came because most of the funding was not needs based or bottom up.

Donors realized that they could not just ride rough shod like *cowboys* and dictate what they wanted to do and how they wanted it done; now they are asking countries to prioritize their needs so they can be given funding accordingly. How does this work? We give you the funding but we help you to spend it and in most cases more than fifty percent of the funding goes to administrative costs. Only a little trickles down to the intended beneficiary in some village who will never hear the name of the donor nor know that the new water tank was given by so and so.

So, of the one million dollars that was supposed to go to some community, only two hundred thousand dollars reached them if they were lucky. If Donors cannot harmonize because each has their conditionality, countries need to decide that they will harmonize and dictate the terms under which they will accept funding.

This though is only feasible through transparency and accountability for every dollar that comes in. External funding needs to be reflected in the national budget and should be in the national budget and there should be a manner of tracking what comes in and where it goes out for the satisfaction of all stakeholders. Under FDA there should always be in the national budget a section of "If then" indicating that if this amount comes in from this source then this is where it will go and the tasks should be flexible enough as to allow for changes and updates which anyone can read. In spite of the huge amounts of dollars that donors may declare that they spent in Africa over the years, not many countries can tell you exactly how much they have received over any period of time. Those who can cannot tell you how much of what they know came in was spent, where or how. Rather, most governments create development agencies in order to create jobs for their youths and those who are retired or wanting to go on safaris to African countries.

Respect for Laws

Laws in general are meant for everyone and not only for some people. In a law-abiding country, no one is above the law. Some people act as if they were untouchable and above the law. Many national and international laws and norms exist on paper and whether Africa respects those laws is another matter.

Africa has had too many meetings, too much talk, a lot of decisions taken but little or no action. What Africa needs now is not even new laws or policies but the implementation and respect of those that are already in place.

Ivan Hoffman, B.A., J.D. says "Something seemed to have shifted some decades ago and part of that something that seemed to shift was that we seemed, collectively, to lose respect for the law". He goes on to define respect for the law as follows:

"This is not merely the adherence to the letter of the law or even to the spirit of the law. That we all must do and thus that is a given. However, merely complying with the law is not the same as respecting the law. Respect for the law of course includes complying with the law but respect for the law goes beyond that threshold. Complying with the law does not of necessity include respecting the law but respecting the law does include complying with the law.

In its simplest incarnation, the difference can be summarized as follows: "Just because you can doesn't mean you should." Respect for the law is not merely, not doing something negative but is actually doing something positive. Respect for the law is behaving in such a way that you act affirmatively to manifest respect for the law. Respect means acting with deference and esteem, even awe for the law, and with a sense that the law has value over and above the immediacy of the application of the law in a given situation. It means that we nurture the law, help the law to evolve and in turn allow the law to help us evolve as well. Without law there can be no civilization. Indeed, it is the law that creates civilization.

Acting affirmatively is much more difficult than merely refraining from action perhaps in large part because it requires us to recognize and in turn manifest a sense of how our own conduct impacts on the totality of all conduct, generally referred to as "society." It is not to be left to others to respect the law, to advance society. The only "others" are we ourselves.

Manifesting an affirmative respect for the law says that you expect to raise the level of discussion to a higher plane, and that you expect others to follow. If all we seek is minimum compliance with the law, then all we will end up with is a minimum compliance world, a world without excellence. We of course want to have a world in which everyone complies with the law. But we deserve a better world than a merely compliant world. Striving to reach a higher goal in our business and legal behaviour can help create a maximum world, a world in which everyone actually respects the law as opposed to a world in which all we have is begrudging compliance.

Demonstrating respect for the law requires modelling appropriate legal behaviour. Merely refraining is not as important a teaching tool - for "society" as well as a more personal level - as is affirmatively modelling. Affirmatively modelling requires us to have the sense that our conduct actually matters in the larger world, in that "society." It often appears that few believe they have any value in the world outside of their own selves. Believing that we are small generally produces people who are small. And thus believing they then act to make their beliefs their truths. Believe small, stay small. Failing to dream creates its own reality.

It is a difficult thing to go against the trend of something as large as society. The tendency often is to "go along to get along." But the difficulty is part of the journey.

The international human rights movement was strengthened when the United Nations General Assembly adopted the Universal Declaration of Human Rights (UDHR) on 10 December 1948. Drafted as 'a common standard of achievement for all peoples and nations', the Declaration for the first time in human history spelt out basic civil, political, economic, social and cultural rights that all human beings should enjoy. It has over time been widely accepted as the fundamental norms of human rights that everyone should respect and protect. International human rights law lays down obligations which States are bound to respect. By becoming parties to international treaties, States assume obligations and duties under international law to respect, to protect and to fulfil human rights. The obligation to respect means that States must refrain from interfering with or curtailing the enjoyment of human rights. The obligation to protect requires States to protect individuals and groups against human rights abuses. The obligation to fulfil means that States must take positive action to facilitate the enjoyment of basic human rights.

Through ratification of international human rights treaties, Governments undertake to put into place domestic measures and legislation compatible with their treaty obligations and duties. Where domestic legal proceedings fail to address human rights abuses, mechanisms and procedures for individual complaints or communications are available at the regional and international levels to help ensure that international human rights standards are indeed respected, implemented, and enforced at the local level.

The UN declaration of human rights has been ratified by all countries, and one would think that that would have been enough, but there are still many offshoots of the law to deal with specific cases like the law for the protection of minorities, children, indigenous people, women etc. If the one declaration of human rights was enforced by all countries with respect to all human beings there would be no need for any other laws to be enacted.

In Cameroon as in many other African countries, so many laws exist but the problem is one of enforcement. For example, there is a certain distance in every country where people are not allowed to build by the highway. However, in most SSA these norms are not respected thus creating problems in the future when time would come to expand roads. Those buildings which were illegally built too close to the highway in the first place will have to be destroyed and even if the government pays or not for the destruction, that would be something that could have been avoided if the laws were respected in the first place.

The respect of law and the existence of an independent and strong judiciary is the hall mark of a society which can attract foreign investors. Cases abound in which the same land has been sold to multiple buyers. There are even cases of multiple land tittles to the same piece of land, all tell-tell signs of loose application and follow up of the law. The consequence is infringement on individual or group rights with attendant consequences of pain, suffering and losses. The story of pickpockets operating under the very nose of the police or conmen working in league with the police superintendents and magistrates are replicated in many African countries. Insecurity is rife and neither nationals nor strangers are secure.

Insecurity in most African countries

Gloomy high fences have replaced the beautiful flower beds and hedges of the sixties and seventies in Africa. Stealing was rare, locks were unheard of and the penalty for stealing was stiff.

Today if you don't see a wall fenced around a house then it is a rare exception. Some fences are higher than the houses and some look like prison fences. The irony is that as these fences go up the rate of broad day light stealing and armed robbery are increasing to the point where there is more insecurity than security even with the fences. This sharply contrasts with developed countries where fences are rare.

In most African countries, there is a correlation between high unemployment rate, poverty and insecurity. The higher the fences the higher the rate of the other factors, yet the fences do not succeed in keeping out those it should keep out or improve the quality of life for those outside the fence looking in. What does development mean in these circumstances? Is it the right of every individual to have his/her basic needs met or the fight for a few to have so much that they need to protect it at an inconvenience or insecurity to themselves? No fence is high enough to keep out determined robbers. Some robbers simply follow the occupants of the houses into the compound and shut the gates behind them, then operate and leave without anyone knowing that anything went on within the fences because no one could see through. Another saddening thing about fences and the so-called development is that in cities people are beginning to live with neighbours they don't even know or talk to. An African child used to belong to the community and any adult could discipline a child they saw going wrong without asking the parents or even telling the parents after. Today, apart from the many distractions for children, there are laws protecting children from being punished even at schools. The things the

African copies from the developed world are not things to help it develop but rather things to keep it from developing and to lose African values in the making.

Culture, Values and Ethics

Culture is what defines a people. It is also what separates people. There is no pure African culture because there has been so much migration and intermarriages that what used to be known and accepted as African culture for a continent too vast and diverse no longer exists. However, African culture as defined by its arts, the languages, lifestyles, food, and the way of looking at life was unique to the continent before the invasion of, first, the Arabs from the North who needed cheap labour and invaded Africa to get slaves and then Europe and the Americans who followed suit to Africa.

Thinkers have defined and analysed *culture* in various ways. Prof. Edward Burnett Tylor, 19th century English anthropologist, gave one of the first clear definitions of *culture* in the West. He defined *culture* as a complex collection of "knowledge, belief, art, law, morals, customs and any other capabilities and habits acquired by man as a member of society". According to Matthew Arnold, a poet of the Victorian era, *culture* means "contact with the best which has been thought and said in the world". He considered *culture* as a "study of perfection". Pt. Jawaharlal Nehru, the first Prime Minister of independent India, described *culture* as the outcome and basis of training, establishment and development of physical and mental potentials.

Anthropologist William A. Haviland in *Cultural Anthropology* holds that:

"Culture is a set of rules or standards that, when acted upon by the members of a society, produce behaviour that falls within a range of variance the members consider proper and acceptable." In other words, culture does not refer to the behaviour that is observed but to values and beliefs which generate behaviour. Some modern definitions of culture tend to be inclusive of the "emerging culture" of society. For instance, in Culture and Modernity, Roop Rekha Verma defines culture as "a system of the patterns and the modes of expectations, expressions, values, institutionalisation and enjoyment habits of people in general."

There are thus many viewpoints on *culture* and the meaning and purpose of *culture* is vast –incorporating the genesis and expansion of the philosophy, values, goals and modes of life in any society or nation. In short, *culture* is the traditional yet evolving basis and nature of life of a social or national system that provides support and atmosphere for civilized, liberal and illuminating progress of people. It is an ensemble of immeasurable trends and attempts that have gradually evolved and excelled since ancient times and have contributed to the overall development and progress of humans. Culture represents those lines of thoughts and systems of the human society that aim to cultivate in every realm of human life[5]. The cultural values and trends of a nation are therefore the foundational elements of its development and strength. The *culture* of a nation is its true wealth.

If the culture of a nation is its true wealth, then we can see why African nations have failed to develop along with the

---

[5] *Samskaras :* The short novel "Samskara" by U. R. Anantha Murthy, professor for English at the Mysore University, created a big furore in Karnataka when it was published more than thirty years ago. With this novel Anantha Murthy, a brahmin himself, held aloft a clear mirror to the brahmin community. He raised the question "What is actually culture (Samskara) - is it achieved by blindly following rules and traditions, is it lost when they are not kept?"
http://www.antiessays.com/free-essays/220534.html

rest of the world. Most African nations no longer have any culture, values or ethics which are truly theirs because in the migration and mixing and swirling of lifestyles and peoples, something fundamental in the African has been lost and that is its culture. Without a culture, how does a society develop its own values? In the loss of its culture, the African perhaps lost hold of reality. Yet reality itself is a hydra.

Without its own values, how does a nation have any ethics? (It is perhaps in place here to pit in on this Lenten sermon of a Catholic priest the first Sunday of Lent March 13, 2011)

The real world: in chat shows and in daily conversations we often hear people talk about 'the real world'. Where is this 'real world'? What is it like? The other expression I hear often in Cameroon is 'A real life situations'. The Cameroonian real life situation or real world is the place where people fiddle and cheat, where infidelity in marriage and over-indulgence in alcohol is the norm. If this is indeed the definition of the real world, then lent is an invitation for us to stay in the unreal world.

Another real world: There is another equally real world; where people try to love God and their neighbour; the world where a fall is followed by repentance; where an argument is followed by an apology. This is the world where being at the top is not the only priority. It is a world where people pay tax, a fair wage, and do an honest day's work. It is a world where people try to be faithful in marriage and where one's word is one's bond.

These two worlds are in competition with one another. The question today is, how can a Christian live in the so-called real world with integrity? (Father Tantoh).

The human being pays allegiance to some god, a supreme being whom they acknowledge as their creator. It does not matter if that Being is called GOD, Allah, the Buddha, Brahma, Vishnu, Shiva or any name the people choose to call him. The important thing is that there is a supreme being about whom the culture, the lives, the ethics and values of every race is built, detected by some force which is stronger than the people.

There is no one size fits all in Africa, but the general culture is one of respect for the elders, honour for ancestors who in most African folk lore never die but cross to the other side and can still be called upon or talked with when things get really bad. Most African societies have forgotten what their cultures, values and ethics were. This does not mean that they cannot, even in a society in which much of its history is oral, go back and find out what it was. Africans do not only need to help them get their identity but to reinforce the fact that they are one people and not obliged to live according to some artificial boundaries drawn up by the same people who enslaved them, divided them and are still dividing them in order to get what they can from us and not to help us.

To be fooled more than once is to be foolish indeed. What is the choice? Does Africa want to be the perennial fool or to be truly self-determined and take its future into its own hands? Africa's past only truly counts if it helps it to make its future better, not if it continues to enslave it. The perceptual difference of leadership in the West and in most of Africa was vividly brought to the fore in the following press reaction to Michelle Obama's trip to Spain:

First lady under fire for her glitzy Spanish vacation
By Holly Bailey holly Bailey – Thu Aug 5, 6:43 pm ET
As her husband celebrated his 49th birthday in Chicago with Oprah, first lady Michelle Obama was halfway around the world, on vacation with her 9-year-old daughter, Sasha, in Spain. The two are traveling on what the White

House has described as a four-day "private trip" with several Obama family friends along the country's ritzy southern coast.

Of course, no first lady's life is truly ever private, and already plenty of drama is swirling around Michelle Obama's foreign jaunt. Some critics have laid into the trip's price, while others are highlighting an apparent diplomatic gaffe between the United States and Spain.

Fox News reports that prior to the first lady's arrival, the State Department had issued a travel warning to Americans advising that "racist prejudices could lead to the arrest of Afro-Americans who travel to Spain." The wording was reportedly removed from the State Department website Monday, ahead of Michelle Obama's arrival in the country Wednesday.

Yet the bigger public furor concerns the cost and appearance of the trip. In a scathing editorial published Thursday, New York Daily News writer Andrea Tantaros trashed Michelle Obama as a "modern day Marie Antoinette" for taking such a glitzy vacation while most of the country is struggling to make ends meet. The Obama entourage is staying at the luxury Hotel Villa Padierna, a Ritz-Carlton property often described as one of the world's top 10 hotels. Rates range between $500 and $2,500 a night. It's not clear that the Obama delegation picked this hotel specifically, or if the Secret Service — which often gets final say over where a protectee stays — made the accommodations call.

Either way, White House Press Secretary Robert Gibbs told reporters that the first lady will pay her personal expenses — as will the friends who are traveling with her. But that only covers a small part of the ultimate expense, given that she has full-time Secret Service protection and has to travel with an entourage of staff. That cost, as well as her travel on board an official Air Force charter plane, is covered by taxpayers.

As the Chicago Sun-Times' Lynn Sweet reports, by the end of the summer, the first lady will have taken eight vacations. That includes a June trip to Los Angeles, where she and her daughters attended the NBA Finals, as well as an upcoming trip to the Florida Gulf Coast next weekend and a 10-day visit to Martha's Vineyard later this month with the president.

Michelle Obama is hardly the only first lady to travel overseas without her husband. Laura Bush and her daughters, Barbara and Jenna, traveled to Africa in 2007, where they went on safari. Yet her trip was regarded as an "official" visit and included several public events. According to the White House, this trip is entirely private, save for a photo-op with the Spanish royal family, who has invited the first lady and her daughter for an official visit.

Do African Leaders ever consider the cost of their traveling on the tax payers and does the tax payers ever think about it? The Michelle Obama article came a few days after President Paul Biya returned to Cameroon, three weeks after attending the 2011, July 14th French celebrations, spent two days in the country and was to leave again on an official visit to Brazil at the end of which he would spend another two to three weeks in transit. The whole government and their spouses turn out at the airport before the presidents' departure and when he returns. Does anyone calculate the costs of all of that to the tax payers? The IMF, World Bank and all development organizations watch all of these and criticize in private but no one dares to say anything in public. The roads are blocked for hours before the President leaves or arrives and no one ever takes the time to look at the cost to the economy and the businesses whose products are being blocked from operating. This is a country in the bottom billion, dreaming of becoming an emerging economy before the end of the 21st century. When the other economies would have made giant leaps again and the distance between developing and emergent would have widened!

How can all these things happen while people look on silently? It is not for lack of people who know the truth.

Rather, it is for lack of people with the guts and the mind set to do something. It is time for Africa and Africans to realize that just as there are no free lunches, there are no situations where development has been promoted from outside. None in the history of man and Africa is not an exception. Another example of differences in culture and attitudes can be seen in the case of appointments versus elections:

When people are appointed to positions of responsibility in Cameroon close relatives, family and friends celebrate the appointment and some drink to stupor. One hears people saying things like *"this is our own time to eat", "haha, if my brother e dei for on top plum tree then me a go chop ripe plum too"* which simply means if my relative is on a plum tree then I too will eat a ripe plum no matter how stingy that relative is, on and on. No one ever stops to ask themselves where the money is coming from for the celebrations and the enormous responsibilities the new position brings to the person and how they can contribute to make that person's job and contribution to the nation and national economy to grow. No one thinks of the implications for expecting to *chop* more than the person is earning and the ramification thereafter.

Then when the person appointed is eventually removed, friends and even some family members (the same ones who were dancing and rejoicing at the appointment and who may have pushed the appointee to live above his means) disappear into thin air. Worse is if the sacked appointee is caught for embezzlement or mismanagement and jailed. The fans and friends fizzle off leaving him/her lonely. Yet the lesson is not learned. Those going in think that they were appointed because they are better than their predecessor and so they are favoured. Only God knows if those going out merited being sacked or not. But as often happens they usually go out not in a blaze of glory but sneak off as if they were criminals.

With appointments the people appointed pay allegiance and worship one individual instead of the electorate. Even with a bad leader as is the case in most failing states, the president's entourage is actually choir singing his praises instead of objectively looking at situations. Both the president and his choir make each other look stupid because no one dares to tell the truth, like in "the kings' cloths". (The king's cloth is a story of a proud monarch who was told by a cloths maker that he would make special cloths for the King which only those people who were pure or holy could see. The rascal brought cloths which no one could see but the King could not admit that he was a sinner so he walked out of the palace and went to public places naked because no one dared to acknowledge that the king was naked until an innocent child called out "The King has no cloths on")

Graduation

The University of Buea alone was graduating 3500 students in a single ceremony which will be repeated in all the other universities. Of the smiling youths who happily receive their diplomas, all but 1% only have short-lived the beautiful smiles. Less than 1% will end up in the job market. The expenditure for the dresses, the party afterwards, transportation and all that goes into the celebrations, wisely considered could be used to start a small business.

The idea of an age limit for integration into the Cameroon public service poses a problem. If anyone wants to work with the government and has even taken the time to pass the entrance into one of the professional schools, the chances are that they will not be integrated into the public service if they are thirty three years of age. After that they have about twenty two years of active service and depending on the core they are sent on retirement. While retirement age in the developed world, is above sixty, in Cameroon and in most African countries the retirement age is less than sixty. For a people who need human resources, retirement just when they are ripe to give all their experience into the state portfolio, is unwise.

Reparation

Africans in America and other developed countries have committed many crimes such as credit card theft, telephone card theft, shoplifting, you name it through some misguided notion that they "The Whiteman owes us". They justify their laziness and misdemeanour with some strange confusion that Africa is owed some form of reparation.

Much talk of reparation, stagnation and the reason Africa has not developed blames the colonial masters. Yes, Africa was colonized and yes, Africans were taken or sold into slavery. African history can never be completely told without this but that past is only valuable if Africans learn from it rather than use it as an excuse for stagnation. Should colonial masters pay Africa for raping her and taking its sons and daughters into slavery? It remains a scar of bitterness that Africans were forced out of their homelands, dehumanized, depersonalized, brutalized and put into serfdom for centuries without any dignity or recognition, treated as objects and left with scars so deep that they have been unable to heal in some families. But can Africans claim total innocence? Who condoned, cooperated and sold their brothers into slavery?

Stealing from the "Whiteman" in some misguided sense that "they owe us" is childish. Africans need to sit at table like adults and look honestly at where Africa is today and where it should be in the next 10, 20, 30, or 50 years. They should choose to be on the economic and social agenda of success. If Africa wants to be counted and respected, continuing to receive hand-outs in the form of aid or even loans is certainly not the way; stealing is dishonest even with patched excuse of "reparation".

Humiliating references to Africa abound. William Easterly calls Africa "The Whiteman's Burden" while Paul Collier says that most countries at the "Bottom Billion" of the world's poorest are in Sub-Saharan Africa. The immorality of criminal behaviour would only add to Africa's shame.

Projections for the next fifty years portray Africa as non-essential and of no consequence in the international political, social, economic and scientific arena. This indictment of Africa may be partially true. While Africa has many more schools, and therefore more educated people than they had at independence, the problem has not been illiteracy but what kind of education is Africa giving its children? What marketable skills does it have?

Added to education, there certainly are more roads, more hospitals, health care centres, portable drinking water and just about everything that is used to determine and indicate progress and development. So, why is Africa not considered a serious contender to development? The reason seems to be that at the time when Africa need not reinvent in any domain its progress can at best be described as lethargic. There is pathos in this because the continent most endowed is the world's poorest.

Electricity

Generators not only pollute the air with noise and carbon monoxide, they are simply a nuisance. However, because of the frequent electrical cuts in most African countries and with the instability of electricity, most wealthy people and businesses have no choice but to own and operate generators. That is why, sometimes in Lagos alone, the cacophony from generators can simply give you a head ache and an ear ache. Africa is blessed with huge waterfalls, rivers with long chutes which could be used for hydroelectricity and serve three or four countries from only one supplier so why is she not using the resources she has? Electricity is not a luxury but a necessity which should be a fundamental right of every citizen.

It was seven in the evening. The night was approaching as I left the conference in Accra with arms load of paper work I was taking home to rest a little and get back to work. I was tired and hungry after an intense day of talking and facilitating a workshop. I walked out and the hot air hit me on the face as if to signal the end of my comfort. Then I looked right then left and everything was dark. There were no lights anywhere.

I got into a cab and as the driver took me to my hotel where I prayed they would have lights, the driver remarked, "This MDGs (Millennium Development Goals) they are laudable, but they are too much for us Africans. Why don't we make our own objectives which are simple and which we can attain?"

"Like what?" I asked

"Like take a small area in the city each year or two and say we will make sure that everyone has water and electricity everyday forever. That way we cover the city bit by bit then move out towards the villages"

I was feeling too morose to have a philosophical discussion with my cab driver but I could not agree more with him. Yet I could not help going back to my early home experience. In those days, we had neither running water nor electricity. But we had a running stream nearby and bush lamps and *Tilley lamps* to light. Having lights depended on us because so long as we had money to buy kerosene (which we always had while my grandfather was alive) we had lights. There was no need of a tap when we had a stream because we had a latrine instead of flush toilets.

The Ghanaian plight repeats itself throughout Africa. Lagos, Nairobi, Yaoundé, etc., there is a constant shortage of electricity and water. The Ghanaian driver's proposition is very sane. Yet policy makers repeat like parrots how with one digit growth rate we are going to become an emerging economy by 2035. We might not be there then but who is fooling who? By what magic? How can people who are unable to meet basic needs pipe out development and the MDGs when the MDGs are too broad and ambitious even for the best intentioned? Are we talking about development for a privileged few or we are talking about development which reaches the masses?

With all the resources available in Africa, the biggest problem is not an inability to be able to deliver these services but an inability to do proper forecast and planning. The cities are growing faster than the planned electrical or water systems. It is the same thing with roads and traffic jams in most of our cities. Roads were not planned for and many cars are allowed to come into the country. If proper records were kept, forecasting would be an easy thing of taking the birth and death rate and extrapolating the growth rate. This then can be used to determine the demand for basic services and therefore providing a high quality of service delivery.

Forecasting, simply put, is seeing or identifying a trend then following it.

- Long term forecast, which is uncertain but indicative of the growth and kinds of services which will be in demand at any given moment in time
- Medium term forecast, which can be seen as the trends change, helps in planning for the services that will be needed where, when and in what quantities
- Short term forecast, based on more accurate estimates because the time limit is short and therefore more accurate.

Forecasts can be used to measure the demand for services such as

Food
Roads
Water
Electricity
Doctors
Nurses
Hospitals
Hospital beds
Schools
Teachers, etc

One would think it is easy to take the birth and death rate and determine the growth rate then use these figures to do our forecasting. But the desire to do so is difficult in a culture where to get any data is like looking for the proverbial needle in a haystack.

CHAPTER 5
RESEARCH, DATA AND STATISTICS

The research policy of every country should be based on their developmental goals. There is so much research that still needs to be carried out on the African continent about Africans and Africa, yet not much of the national budgets of most countries are devoted to research. Research is the key to improve on what others have developed and contextualize. Every country needs a good database and research facility in any sector to be able to do proper forecasting and planning. A proper database and research should provide adequate information for planning in each sector of the economy which needs to be developed. Thus, research to document viable statistics is not a luxury for any country but a necessity.

1. **Planning:** These are steps to meet short term needs because they are certain and so investment is certain. Proper forecasting also enables a country to do medium as well as long term planning in all its relevant areas for development.

2. **Implementation**: After good planning, the next thing is to put together the resources to implement the project. Resources include human, material, financial and technical resources.

3. **Maintenance**: Implementing the project does not end there. Maintenance needs to be built into the process of planning and forecasting. A look at most public infrastructure indicates the failure to plan for

maintenance given the state of the infrastructure a few years down the road.

From the appellation *underdeveloped countries* to *developing countries* to *emerging countries* nothing changes in either the perception or situation of the country. The fundamental question is where the country should be. It is unfortunate that some countries regress and should in reality be called stagnant countries or even regressing economies. Many countries at "the Bottom billion", in conflict situations, or just coming out of conflict or conflict situation are in this category. Some countries have very unstable economies, with long serving dictators toting a small choir singing their praises and lying to them that the country is doing well even while the vast majority is on the brink of starvation. There are at the stage of regressionism or can be called failing states as Collier puts it.

TRADE

Trade by barter was crude, it was not convenient, but people went to the market and left satisfied with whatever they got. Today we talk of fair trade but the balance of trade deficit of the bottom billions vis-a-vis the developed world is negative which means that the bottom billions will stay poor and indebted to the rich nations for long. To reverse the situation Africa's exports must be more than its imports until such a time that Africa is at parity. The only way to do that is to increase its production of basic needs and add value to its natural resources before exportation. Africa has to return to the drawing board, re-evaluate its educational systems and plan to have the skills necessary to do the transformation. As to whether there should be an African monetary union, the answer should be a resounding yes. With the hedge of a monetary union Africans would be forced to cooperate and help each other to develop and maximize their opportunity cost and returns on investment and also benefit from economies of scale.

Beatrice Fri Bime

According to the UNCTAD (United Nations Conference on Trade and Development) report, Africa's share in global exports in value terms increased only marginally, from 2.3 to 2.8 per cent between 2000 and 2006. Mr. Cheick Sidi Diarra[6] said: "While globalization has brought prosperity and better income distribution to many parts of the world, the benefits of globalization have failed to reach the overwhelming majority of the population in Sub-Saharan Africa."

There are enormous trade potentials to assist African countries in their development efforts. Therefore, the creation of an equitable and transparent multilateral trading system is imperative if Africa plans on reaching its MDGs. Special attention needs to be given to issues of particular concern to Africa, *inter alia*, market access for agricultural goods, reduction in tariff peaks and escalation, reduction in market-distorting export subsidies and domestic support measures, and preference erosion.

As globalization advances, the majority of countries in Sub-Saharan Africa are lacking the starting point that would allow them to participate more effectively in world trade, such as access to basic transport and communications infrastructure, skilled human resources, developed private sector and strong institutional frameworks. Moreover, constantly changing global markets, where many sectors are dominated by resource rich and technologically advanced corporations, have made it extremely difficult for small enterprises and new players from African countries to be competitive.

Therefore, trade-related capacity building is key to increasing the competitiveness of African countries and

---

[6] Under-Secretary-General, Special Adviser on Africa and High Representative for the Least Developed Countries, Landlocked Developing Countries and Small Island Developing States on "Trade and Development for Africa's Prosperity: Action and Direction" during the high-level segment UNCTAD XII Conference, Accra, Ghana, 21 April 2008

ensuring their beneficial integration into the world economy. To that end, building productive capacities, development of physical infrastructure, human capital, and strong institutions are crucial for sustained growth and sustainable development of African countries.

At the same time, national ownership and leadership in designing a successful export-led growth strategy for Africa need to be emphasized. Trade needs to become a bigger part of national development strategies. African countries need to further improve the business climate, remove critical supply-side constraints, build productive capacity and enhance product quality. Moreover, considering that many African countries are dependent on exports of single commodity, upgrading from primary commodity exports through diversification of products and exports remains an important challenge. In the right environment, the private sector could thrive. The importance of a vibrant private sector as an engine for growth, job creation and poverty reduction, is now widely recognised" If every country wants to have a positive balance of payment, most economies would be stressed. However, trade has to be done in such a way as to make it a win-win situation for everyone.

- A need to educate the public about the benefits of foreign investments and the benefit of integrating the nation's economy with the global economy
- Policy and government commitment is key to development and implementing a good foreign direct investment environment

Foreign Direct Investment

Jeffrey P. Graham and R. Barry Spaulding writing on *Understanding Foreign Direct Investment (FDI)* in an article published on the defunct Citibank international business portal said:

Beatrice Fri Bime

Foreign direct investment (FDI) plays an extraordinary and growing role in global business, because it can provide a firm with new markets and marketing channels, cheaper production facilities, access to new technology, products, skills and financing. For a host country or the foreign firm which receives the investment, it can provide a source of new technologies, capital, processes, products, organiza-tional technologies and management skills, and as such can provide a strong impetus to economic develop-ment. Foreign direct investment, in its classic definition, is defined as a company from one country making a physical investment into building a factory in another country.

Their research also found that the most profound effect has been seen in developing countries, where yearly foreign direct investment flows have increased from an average of less than $10 billion in the 1970's to a yearly average of less than $20 billion in the 1980's, to explode in the 1990s from $26.7billion in 1990 to $179 billion in 1998 and $208 billion in 1999 and now comprise a large portion of global FDI. Driven by mergers and acquisitions and internationalization of production in a range of industries, FDI into developed countries last year rose to $636 billion, from $481 billion in 1998 (Source: UNCTAD), however, Proponents of foreign investment point out that the exchange of investment flows benefits both the home country (the country from which the investment originates) and the host country (the destination of the investment). Opponents of FDI note that multinational conglomerates are able to wield great power over smaller and weaker economies and can drive out much local competition.

Given the stated argument, the question is can FDI contribute to the economic development of Africa? The answer would be yes if the following conditions are met:

- The African market in general is a large growing sophisticated market. Consumers are educated and discerning. As such, the products they desire should meet certain standards.

- The perception that African countries are a great risk due to corruption and instability is reduced in the eyes of foreign investors.
- FDI must and should create wealth for both countries. It should create economic and social value for both countries for a win-win for both countries.
- The resources needed for the FDI to work should be available; an educated and skilled work force, infrastructure, and enabling environment.
- The government therefore needs to put in place the mechanisms to foster foreign direct investment. Both foreign and national partners should feel secure and protected in case of a disagreement.

Therefore it does not matter who Africa's trade partners are; Europe, America, or Asia. If there is no fair price for Africa's goods and services because Africa can neither transform them nor bargain well or compete, then Africa's development will not happen through trade.

The problem is thus not Africa's trading partners. The problem is Africans themselves. When OPEC (**Organization of the Petroleum Exporting Countries**) decided to raise prices in the late 70s, the consumers had no choice but to pay the fair prices which the exporting countries were asking. They could only do that from a position of strength by coming together in a very strong union. What is wrong with Africa emulating that example?

Trading Across Borders

Proponents of One Africa say that there should be no borders in Africa as exhibited in the AU emblem. However, that will be an argument with no winners yet. How do the regional bodies fare?

When I travel within the country and see customs posts, I ask myself what is it they are doing there and most often it is to ensure that imported goods are paid for. The question I ask is if they were not paid for how would they have arrived inside the country? Why do I have to produce a customs receipt for something which I paid for in the local market and am just transporting it from one region to another?

The World Bank "Doing Business" 2010 report states that the benefits of trade are well documented as are the obstacles to trade. The same report goes on to say that with bigger ships and faster planes the world is shrinking, yet Africa's trade today is smaller than it was 25 years ago. Nothing wrong with studying philosophy and theology but in today's global world, diversification is central. Today's African should be able to think outside the box and should not be glued to the governments' apron strings like a desperate pauper. Africans need to break the dependency cycle and crack out the cocoon of the ostrich policy. There is no denying it that many spend energies on the wrong things or as someone has graphically put it, people spend time singing beautifully outside the choir. If there is one thing today's world so desperately needs it is undeniably integrity. The world yearns badly for men of honour, men imbued with the sense of shame. In a world starving for people of character, the challenge then to Africans is to be salt to the earth and light to the world.

Aid versus Trade

In international relations, aid is defined as a voluntary transfer of resources from one country to another, given at least partly with the objective of benefiting the recipient country.

The same paper goes on to say that development aid is aid given by developed countries to support development in general which can be economic development or social development in developing countries. It is distinguished from humanitarian aid as being aimed at alleviating poverty in the long term, rather than alleviating suffering in the short term.

Aid is seldom given from motives of altruism; rather they are tied to conditionality's which favour the giving country. For instance, aid may come with the clause that only companies from the giving country should execute the aid. Expatriates come in with the aid even if cheaper local labour and expertise exists. Sometimes aid is given as an incentive to change or direct policies in the recipient country.

Given the above, it is obvious that aid is not a recommended strategy for Africa because aid breeds dependency and dependency leads to complacency, which accommodates laziness, excuses, abuses and indifference.

There is strong evidence that no nation or continent can be developed by unhealthy people. Yet Africa's resources to fight against its three pandemic; HIV and aids, tuberculosis and malaria including other diseases comes from foreign aid. If Africa's health depends on external factors just as everything else, it becomes a given that Africa will never develop. In any case, is the giver a sincere one? Has the West really changed or been converted? What makes Africans believe that the same people who killed their gods, defiled their lands, abused and raped their women, stole and enslaved their youths, fanned and encouraged pilferage, looting and wars have suddenly changed? Has the West changed its attitudes, beliefs and arrogance and will now help Africa to develop? Who has convinced Africans that they can trust their slave masters and not each other? Who has told Africans that their languages split their ears but that foreign languages will bring them closer to globalization?

The Executive Director of one aid organization focused on financing health programmes in Africa was heard to have said in 2004 while visiting south Africa to visit one of the programmes that "...If you hold your nose, it's amazing what you can bear". If you imagine that this was said in South Africa the most developed Sub-Saharan African country then you can imagine what he could have said in another African country. Yet, he was earning hundreds of thousands of US dollars for channelling money to bring wellness to Africa.

My old illiterate grandmother used to look at what African leaders are doing and asked: Can someone serve you who has no respect for you? That was the wisdom of age. No one gains respect who is sleeping. Respect is earned. Wake up Africa. It's time to fight another kind of battle. Your forefathers slept while the yellow one raped her.

> They had eyes but could not see;
> Ears but could not hear;
> Mouth but could not speak,
> Brains but could not think,
> Strength but could not fight.

Africa's dependency on foreign aid can only make it vulnerable and stunt its own growth. Many AIDS infected people today are alive because their governments are receiving foreign funds to supply them with care and treatment. But during a financial crisis or depression such as that which has hit the world the funds are reduced or stopped. How many African countries put in place measures for sustainability?

Aid in whatever form is a gift. With every gift comes a responsibility. However, African countries do not yet understand the notion that when they receive aid instead of being happy and complacent because someone else has shouldered their short term problems, they should breathe a little and make strategic plans for the future. They sit there and, without appreciation, continue living their lives as if they had nothing to worry about except eating and making merry.

Because of the loud cry for free and fair trade, UNTACD was created by the UN general assembly in 1964 to promote the development-friendly integration of developing countries into the world economy. UNCTAD has progressively evolved into an authoritative knowledge-based institution whose work aims to help shape current policy debates and thinking on development, with a particular focus on ensuring that domestic policies and international action are mutually supportive in bringing about sustainable development.

The organization works to fulfil this mandate by carrying out **three key functions**:

- It functions as a **forum for intergovernmental deliberations**, supported by discussions with experts and exchanges of experience, aimed at **consensus building**.
- It undertakes **research, policy analysis and data collection** for the debates of government representatives and experts.
- It provides **technical assistance** tailored to the specific requirements of developing countries with special attention on the needs of the least developed countries and of economies in transition. When appropriate, UNCTAD cooperates with other organizations and donor countries in the delivery of technical assistance.

Many years later, a lot of money having been spent on administrative overheads, there is no semblance of free or fair trade between African countries and their allies. Actually, the futures contracts signed by desperate African ministers or Presidents leave a lot to be desired. Oil lease is signed for 99 years at $9 a barrel? After most countries signed many of such leases, according to a World Bank report, the price of oil shot up to over $90 a barrel. Can the leases or the contracts not be revised, broken or re-negotiated? What kind of a contract cannot be broken or re-negotiated? Who is fooling who? What is the role of UNCTAD and where are the fair trade policies in such contracts? One would have thought that the oil companies or nations could be sued for malpractice, fraud or deceit. But no, the colonial past cannot let go and African countries are too cowardly to do any such thing. Just where is the policy of decency or fairness in this situation?

POWER

Those in power are blinded by greed, self-interest and the maintenance of the status quo because it benefits them so they refuse to see beyond their noses. How would anyone in government who has never paid a private visit (I mean without the people knowing) in the rainy season to a remote village understand the state of the road or the level of poverty of the people? How would someone who has a choice of different plates of food four times a day everyday understand the plight of someone who cannot afford a meal a day let alone one balanced meal? How would someone who has an unlimited financial source at their fingertips understand the anxiety of someone who has never had the pleasure of holding a ten thousand francs note in his hands let alone use it? How would someone who does not know how much, where and when bills are paid understand the man who is in dire straits because he cannot pay his bills? How can someone who is surrounded by guards understand the man who is afraid because of insecurity? How can any man who has never lacked electricity understand the needs of the poor villager who cannot venture outside his door at night because it's too dark for him to see? How can anyone who has never known suffering and pain understand the suffering and pain of others? Even some who have been close to some of these things quickly forget once they are in power. Meanwhile they resort to serving themselves and expect to be served.

CHAPTER 6

WOMEN AND DEVELOPMENT

The Traditional African Women and Power

The West came to Africa and spread the myth that the African was unruly and that women had no power. Individual exceptions may abound but collectively in most of Africa, women have always participated in decision making and power sharing at the level of their different Kingdoms.

I will take the example of Cameroon which can apply to the rest of the continent. In the Western regions of Cameroon, the Queen mothers called by various names in the different Fondoms wielded a lot of power in the choice of a Fon and the way the Fondom was run. Hardly any englobing decision could be taken without consulting the Queen mother or *Ma'fon*. These women, together with other women's secret societies, held religious, economic and political power. They actively participated in the crowning of the Fons, Kings or chiefs and made decisions that enhanced nation building, kept peace and restored harmony to the community and intervened during inter-tribal wars.

In the economy women have always been full actors as farmers or traders as some even worked to pay their husbands taxes to the government or council. Examples abound of women who have brought about change in many communities. In 1931, Douala women marched to the Governor's palace to protest a tax which the colonial master, Germany had placed on their husbands and the Germans had no choice but to lift the tax. The women would have had to pay the tax for their husbands but the burden these would have placed on their families was not negligible.

In Kom in the Bamenda highlands, between 1940 -1950 the *Anlu* women led a ferocious fight against the British for the control of their land and also played a major role in independence politics.

In most African countries lineage is paternal and not matrilineal. Child upbringing in most cases, however, is the responsibility of the mother not that of the father. So if sons and daughters turn into responsible adults the credit is due to women, and vice versa. Women will have to wake up, stretch out and take on additional responsibility of contributing towards getting Africa out of poverty and towards development. This is not just because men have failed but because all, including women, have contributed towards making men take off their eyes from the goal and not prioritize their achievements. In a society where women are responsible for raising children, what the children become in later life cannot be divorced from their upbringing at home. The family is the nucleus of society and good family leads to a good society because that is where we all first learn moulding values.

The African family has been an extended one since time immemorial. No wonder that one of the fabrics of the African society, its extended family, is what the Whiteman or its distractors target to ruin. That is exactly what they are gunning for. Ruin the family fabric and ruin the united national structure.

The Role of the Women in the Economies Moving in the Right Direction

South Africa which is an emerging economy has 45% of women in parliament while Rwanda, in spite of the wounds of the genocide, has 56.3% of women in parliament actually leading the statistics of women in parliament worldwide, and

Angola 38% of women in parliament. The statistics of women in key government positions in 2012 in Africa are as follows: one female head of state, a female Secretary General at the AU, 5 ministers of finance in Guinea-Bissau, Burundi, Uganda (2), Liberia and Benin. Other women in key government positions are Ministers of Defense in Cape Verde, Madagascar, São Tomé et Príncipe, South Africa, Gabon and Botswana. At the ministry of foreign Affairs, there are 8 representing Rwanda, Guinea-Bissau, South Africa, Malawi, Mauritania, Rwanda, Niger and Madagascar. Thus women in cabinet positions are on the rise but not enough to be meaningful.

There does seem to be a correlation between increased participation of women in government, parliament and leadership roles with development. During the 2008 international women's day the ILO ran a campaign which read "Employing women is not only right, but smart". How many African countries are smart or want to be smart? Women need to come out, and not only register to vote but also be at the forefront of development.

ASIANS

A Zambian girl got married to a Chinese man, after two months in the new marriage she got pregnant and duly bore a baby girl who died; at the funeral the Aunt came crying. `I KNEW IT, `I KNEW IT, `IKNEW IT, `I KNEW IT! So close relatives got curious, took the Aunt by the side and in a quest to establish what she knew. Then she said loudly, `I KNEW IT, THOSE CHINESE PRODUCTS DON'T LAST!!!!!!

For the African this joke is sadly true not because all Chinese products are bad or substandard. After all most American and European countries sub contract a lot of their production to their companies in China. However, while they do so and determine and set the standards of production, most African countries have no standards and no quality control measures in place so the things the Chinese send to Africa are the rejects of the other countries. And what they send is equal to the value which the African is willing to pay. In order to be fully satisfied with the Chinese, one has to know exactly what one wants, ensure that the specifications are in the contract with the Chinese and that both sides understand what is being agreed on in order to have satisfaction and quality. The responsibility for Africa again devolves on the African state's quality control. When proper quality controls are in place, then it really would not matter where African imported goods are coming from. Until then, Africa will keep receiving and accepting sloppy products and jobs from its new Asian friends.

When Asians go abroad, they take their attire with them. They go to learn as much as they can from the Whiteman, they learn their language, their science and everything that can help them, in their life. They stick together, open shops to cater for their interests and reject the Whiteman's culture and preserve their identity. The African, on the other hand, goes out, abandons his/her own culture, becomes like the Whiteman, learns the Whiteman's language and his habits but fails to learn the things he left his home land to go and learn. The Chinese shop only in Chinese shops and would walk miles to get an item from one of their shops when they could get the article from the corner shop. They believe not only in supporting their kind but in keeping the money circulating amongst them.

It does not really matter who propels Africa towards development so long as it is done in a fair and transparent manner where everyone wins and not in a scheme where the top is trying to cheat on the bottom in order to keep the bottom last and least.

There can be winners all round if prices are fair. But this needs technicians to identify, quantify and evaluate the value of Africa's natural resources. The million dollar question is how possible this can be when, fifty years after independence, hundreds of years after knowing what the

Whiteman wants from its soil, Africa still has to depend on the same people wanting to reap the harvest to be the ones to tell us what we have and how to harvest it. The story goes round of an exploration company which came to Cameroon to explore. They went into the exploration site, worked tirelessly for a couple of months and finally brought a report of the quantity of minerals they estimated could be found on the site. When they took their report to the ministry, one Cameroonian advised them to reduce the quantity so that the company would not have to pay too much tax. Sure enough the advice was taken!

The best thing to do is to make a conditionality of technological transfer where any company that comes to do mining, trains so many nationals in the procedure. Countries should encourage and provide scholarships for young people to go out and learn all of these technologies. When there is no transparency and accountability rumours grow, go around and distort the truth. When the Chinese for instance were building the Yaoundé Conference centre in Cameroon did they or didn't they find huge amounts of diamonds which they mined and took to their home country? The story went round that to escape detection they fabricated huge coffin-like trunks and claimed to be repatriating their dead!

Many people argue that due to its size alone, and the pace at which China, India, Korea and the other Asian countries are developing, any country which wants to develop will have to reckon with them. Yet it cannot be gainsaid that partnership with these must keep clear of the past. The new partnership should not mean simply changing one master for another and playing the game on an uneven play field while the rules of the game remain the same. Africa should either adapt to the rules of the game, change the rules to give it an edge, or change the field. Africa fails to see that in having the products it needs it has both the knife and the yams in its hands but does not know how to use them. Does Africa need a teacher here or just a decision that it can and sure would be able to do so? The challenge for Africa is to make up its mind that it truly wants to develop and then try to do so. Until it does and really realizes that no one can come from outside and propel Africa towards development and help Africa alleviate poverty, then there really is no hope for African Development. The only thing which will be certain will be that there will be pockets of developments which will not amount to much and they will keep Africa many centuries behind their counterparts who started the walk at the same time. But while the Whiteman has been to the moon many times and back, the African is still trekking to the village unsure of when he will reach his destination.

As said earlier, there is no denying that there has been some development in Africa in the last fifty years. It is not true to claim that the level of development in most African countries is up to the level of its expectations or according to the potential available on the continent. The problem with Africa's development process is that despite pockets of achievements and laudable development, the rest of sub Saharan Africa remains the poorest continent in the world and at the pace at which it is going, the gap grows daily between developed, emerging and regressing economies. Statistically, the best African countries are developing at 3.5 to 8% per annum while the rest of the world is developing at double digits. At the pace at which Africa is going, it either has to tie the hands of the other economies at zero development rates in order to catch up in the next 100 years or the gap continues to widen rather than close.

Closing the gap, however, is not a difficult task because unlike the other economies, Africa does not need to reinvent the wheel; all it needs is to learn and emulate good practices from the other economies. The current emerging economies like the Asian countries were at a lesser place than Africa. Fifty years ago the odds of them becoming developed were stacked against them. They lacked natural resources, and human resources but their determination not to be left behind, their willingness to learn and copy, to work hard and get the essentials propelled them to where they are today.

CHAPTER 7

AFRICA IN A GLOBALIZED WORLD: WHAT HAS CHANGED?

With the advent of globalization there is more access to information, especially with the growth of various communication tools: the internet, cell phones and social networks. Africa has not been left unaffected by the communication boom. The communication boom has not changed much for Africa and the African however. If anything, globalization just means that politics stays the same way but the numbers of players have increased while the rules of the game have not changed. The target is still "Self-interest" "raison d'état" and the spoils are oil, minerals, precious stones and other peoples' national resources.

The developed world may preach development and democracy, but this is only so far as it represents their countries' interest and democracy in any place is given to anyone who will protect their interest or maintain the status quo. The fight for the new world no longer depends on finders' being keepers but on wit and might. I want gold, there are large deposits of them somewhere, I make friends with that country and sign conventions which are not fair. After all the fools on whose soil the gold or diamonds are found do not know what it is worth. Most do not know what diamonds look like. Is it any wonder then that Naomi Campbell who comes from the continent can receive gifts of the precious stones from Former Sierra Leonean President Charles Taylor and does not even know what there are or what there are worth? How does the civil servant in his office in the capital city or the villager who has no interest in the whole thing know the value of what those "white people" are wasting their time digging from the ground?

The game today should be played on an even field called fair trade. But how can there be fair trade when the other guy is indifferent and does not and hardly understands the rules of the game? How can fair trade exist when the person who wants what the other has, has all the cards staked in his favour? How can the real owner be treated fairly when he himself does not know what fairness means?

What are the short, medium and/or long term developmental goals? To get everyone's standard of living improved by properly distributing the national cake? To get everyone's basic needs met or provided for? To make the environment enabling for self-development and the acquisition of wealth? To have a strong and independent judicial system where everyone is equal under the law and where everyone is given a speedy and fair trial, irrespective of their station in life? This sounds utopian, but if development is all of these and more, and one person can provide it for his/her country and citizens, then long live progressive dictators. Democracy, especially in the developing world, should not be democracy for its own sake but for the sake of genuine change and progress.

What is repulsive and unacceptable is the dictator who oppresses his people and amasses wealth which he stacks in Swiss Banks while his nation dies because citizens cannot afford simple aspirin for fever or headache. The worst of them all are those dictators who are indifferent to the country and just sit there and watch the country go to the devil while they gallivant all over the world.

Sometimes by 5:30 a.m. Gendarmes and policemen line up the road when the President is scheduled to travel at midday. So why do they have to be out so early? Is it true that the forces of lawlessness use the occasion to earn overtime in which even their boss shares? In Cameroon everywhere people have come up with various ways of getting extra legitimate or illegitimate money. What a people and beloved country even in its disorder!

A foreign diplomat who was on mission in Yaoundé and could not leave his hotel to go to the airport to catch his plane because of one of those famous road blocks for hours before the president was due to travel was heard to say "There has to be something wrong if the roads have to be blocked for so many hours. Either somebody is not doing their jobs or there is no coordination between the police, the gendarmes and the presidential guards" Perhaps all are wrong, a potpourri of armed disorder!

Land

Land makes or identifies a country. Yet most African countries, like Cameroon whose national anthem pays allegiance to land, have no respect for the land. There has been so much migration over the years that national boundaries are fine but they should not delimit citizenship in Africa, especially where the boundaries today were drawn up by foreign powers without taking into consideration culture or relationships and history. The Douala and Bakwerians of Cameroon are one people but one was kept in French-speaking Cameroon while the other was held in English-speaking Cameroon. The Grass fields' dwellers too are one but the same division took place. Yoruba, Togo and Benin are one but today they belong to three different countries. Ghanaians, Ivoirians, and Burkinabe's should be one country, just as most of the CEMAC zone are the same people. Foreign boundaries have been so entrenched that people need visas to go into each other's countries and treat each other as strangers, whereas the languages and background are the same. The map of Africa should be redrawn to indicate one continent, the same people, no countries and no borders.

The map of a United Africa should be redrawn to look like this to indicate one continent, the same people, no countries and no borders.

It is perhaps a pipe dream to think that any President would like to give up their power and their sovereignty in order to unite and form a bigger and stronger Africa. Yet this exercise shows that Africans have more in common with one another than they know or like to believe. More tie Africans together than that which separates its people. Armed with this knowledge, Africans' should stop petty rivalries and instead work together to develop their continent.

Within countries the dispute over land often leads to conflict. Sometimes the piece of land they fight over is so small as to call to question the sanity of the fighters and their priorities. Is that piece of land that one tribe needs to farm worth more than the lives of the people who fight and die for it? Why can't Africans learn to live in harmony? Yet the sources of conflict are often man-manifested. It is often people working in the Lands department who falsify land titles and their compensation is often part of the land which they quickly sell and then ask the buyers to build on it. Having to go to court and spend a lot of money to recover what is rightly one's through lengthy court procedures and many visits to the site is strenuous and very annoying. The phenomenon of double-selling land in cities is found almost everywhere in Africa. These land issues do not make the investment climate conducive for nationals let alone foreigners. Development cannot be achieved without investments in all the sectors, executed by both national and foreign investors in addition to capital. The bail out of this grim situation can reasonably be done by a free, fair, transparent and independent judicial system. This is what most investors are looking for because that is what is conducive to investment.

Investment cannot happen in a climate without fair justice:
- The Judiciary has to be free and fair, fast and independent
- There is a need for in-house cleaning through change of policies, implementing the good ones that are in place, revising what needs revising, ensuring security of persons, goods, services and property
Promoting tourism will only thrive in a climate where people are not harassed and when they feel that they can be protected, safe and sound.

Who is an African?

I come from a mixed background that is all African. My biological father is an Igbo man from Umuahia who at the time of my birth was an Agricultural Engineer working in the Agric farm in Bambui. My maternal grandmother comes from Baba II while her husband, my maternal grandfather, is a Santa Prince whose mother is from Baforchu. They all speak the same vernacular and have the same roots and because of all the chieftaincy relationships in all three villages, I am related to almost everyone from these villages. I lived in Nigeria for a short while when I was young, but I am otherwise a Cameroonian in every sense of the word. I feel Cameroonian and know I am Cameroonian. But I prefer to tell people or just to look at myself as African, full stop. There is actually more that binds Africans together than what separates them, and this includes foreign languages and religion.

Once I was talking with my brother in-law about religion and he asked me "why I should worry about religion when the only reason I am a Christian is because the Europeans came by sea and reached my parents first while the Arabs came on horseback and converted the Northern part of Africa into Islam. So you see it is all a question of where I am found; nothing to do with who I am fundamentally".

I have thought about this remark over the years and as I see the religious killings taking place in Nigeria, I cannot but agree even more and feel sorry for all those who are doing the killing and all those who have lost their lives. Has anyone really taken the time to analyse the facts that not only are we not asking why we are fighting over someone else's religion but that we are praying to the same God?

United African States

The striking affinity of the embassies of many African countries is smallness and dirt. The question to ask is whether they should exist at all. Some are located in dirty small offices with very few staff having little to do. Yet they all cost the various countries a lot of money to run, money which could have been better put to use in health or education. So why can't African countries through the African Union have embassies abroad that represent Africa? The embassies can be arranged according to regional groups with countries sending individual personnel and rotating the position of Ambassador. That would reduce costs across the board. They would send people there who can sell the region or the continent. The vast Canada, the mighty and populous America and even the European Union are doing what Africa ought to be doing in terms of embassy representation. How these wealthy countries know the tricks of time, resource and money saving cuts and the wretched of the earth ignore these advantages!

When one looks at the population of the United States of America and the number of states it represents with the smallest state bigger than most African countries, one wonders why that cannot be done in Africa.

Founding Fathers

In the 1960s when most of Africa was asking for independence they seemed ready for democracy as ideas were shared from door to door. Now half a century later, with more educated people and systems in place, Africa does not seem ready for democracy and self-rule. Underdevelopment and failing states provide the United Nations and other organizations their raison d'être. So, is it in their interest to have development take place at all?

Africa's founding fathers must be turning in their graves to see what has become of what they fought for and lost many lives in the process. Africa needs new leaders, patriotic leaders, lovers of Africa, who genuinely want to see Africa develop. Africa needs Leaders who think of their countries and people not themselves and their families, Leaders like Julius Nyerere, Nelson Mandela, Jerry Rawlings and Gadhafi:

JULIUS NYERERE: *One of Africa's most respected figures, Julius Nyerere (1922 – 1999) was a politician of principle and intelligence. Known as Mwalimu or teacher he had a vision of education and social action that was rich with possibility.*

The first Tanzanian President after independence genuinely believed rightly or wrongly, that the best way to share the national cake equitably was through socialism. His children went to school like other children by bus. He had no special amenities and put the people through a lot of hardship and it is said that when the young "Ali Mazrui" pointed out to him that the route he had taken for his country was bringing untold suffering to his people rather than the development Nyerere thought he was bringing. The President was able to repeat what the young Ali had told him in private in public in front of other Presidents. Then, afterwards he invited the young man to come and explain exactly what he meant and received him in private. When Ali convinced him that the socialist policies he had chosen had brought untold misery to his people, Nyerere resigned, brought democracy to Tanzania and today Tanzania is one of those countries that is closing the gap and is on the right path towards development. The humility to accept that he erred and voluntarily stepped down from power is an unparalleled precedence in African leadership. Only one who truly loves his country could do that. When Julius Nyerere died, the number of dignitaries who came from around the world beat in number and variety any spectacle of the kind on the African continent. They came out of the respect they had for the man.

NELSON MANDELA: Many books have been written about Nelson Mandela and films have been made about his life. Nelson Mandela is an epitome of endurance. He believed in something and fought for it with everything he had- not for himself but for his people. When other people would have been vengeful, he forgave his tormentors. He kept to promises he made. He became the first black South African President and unlike most African heads of states instead of trying to hold on to power, he realized he had nothing more to prove or achieve and gave up power after one term. He made sure his transition was smooth and set the pace for the most developed Sub Saharan African country to continue towards development. What more can a people ask for?

JERRY RAWLINGS: Among Ghanaians there are those who praise Jerry Rawlings and those who do not credit him with much. Yet, he remains one of the few modern day Leaders who has propelled his country out of poverty and put it on a good footing to becoming an emerging economy. He did not do so by sitting in his office and waiting for other people to give him reports of what they were doing; what was happening or not happening. Jerry Rawlings was a hands-on Manager who took World Bank loans and succeeded in doing what the loan was meant for by following every penny of the loan to make sure that the money was properly used. There is a story that he took a loan to build a road and when the World Bank team came for the evaluation, they met Jerry Rawlings right on the road shirt sleeves rolled up working with the people constructing the road. True or false, the fact that the man realized that to whom much is given much is expected and the fact that he understood that being a President meant you had to serve and not to be served makes him an imitable Leader for other African leaders.

MUAMMAR ABU MINYAR AL-GADDAFI: In the USA in the 1980s there was a lot of negative publicity about Gaddafi. Sudan and Ethiopia were starving due to war in one country and drought in the other. The pictures of Africa that were portrayed were of skeletal human beings who were ready to eat the faeces of equally starved cattle. Among the pictures was the pathos of a child continuing to suck at its dead mother's breast. That was the sad Africa of the American press hype although Cameroon and most of the other African countries were not symptomatic of what was being portrayed.

Gaddafi deserves our cheers if he was hated because he stood up to Western prejudice. It does seem that he was hated because he developed his country, redistributed the nation's wealth to its citizens, a thing other African Leaders should copy. His people actually had free water and electricity! Was Gaddafi a bad leader because he could sponsor his citizens to the best schools in the world with decent scholarships for them to live on and did not have to beg or slave for the slave master? We need more leaders like him in Africa.

Granted, the colonel as a human being certainly had his good as well as his bad points. As an African leader and head of state, he certainly did more for his country and people than many of the white boot licking stooges all over the continent have done. Once in a while he had his "cinq minutes de folie" as phrased in Cameroon parlance – He may even have some *Etone* blood in him – Yet he was always willing to extend a helping hand to his neighbours who, because of all the western media hype, were wary of the man.

Many more leaders, with guts like Gaddafi would speed Africa to self-determine and decide to swim by ourselves without help from anyone. Africa can stand up to its partners and, without asking to be treated with respect, respected even if grudgingly. It can ask for fairer prices for its commodities and take an attitude of "take it or leave it" and won't cry over it. It can build its own roads; build its own airports and railways without asking for loans from anyone. Africa can dictate the pace, call the shots and by might stand up to be counted without having to force the issue. Respect is earned, not forced or begged. Africa can, if it decides it can.

Recent events in the Arab world that took Libya in the toll are not an indication that Gaddafi was a bad leader. The indication is rather that no matter how good a leader is human beings like and need change, and a Leader can overstay his welcome. His intentions and policies may even still be good, but after a while, with age and time, there is nothing new to add.

In proof of the initial good intentions and policies of Gaddafi, the United Arab Emirates under the leadership of Sheikh Zayed bin Sultan Al Nahyan who ruled Abu Dhabi from 1966 to 2004 formed the seven member UAE states in 1971. The policy was framed on Gaddafi's Libyan regime whereby oil wealth was redistributed by building infrastructure from houses to hospitals and inviting their citizens to move from the desert into the towns. Today UAE has one of the highest per capita incomes in the world and is poised to be one of the most developed areas of the world.

African Union

Colonization was an evil thing. The Whiteman divided Africa to rule it. They divided Africa without consideration for social or ethnic pluralities. Africa is a continent of small, diverse fragmented countries which should not be countries by any definition of the word. All that has happened is a vital part of the African past and present but it does not have to be its future. Many people who died fighting for African independence are probably turning in their graves and asking themselves why they gave up their lives. They wonder what it was they fought for if the countries are still standing on the same spot, or actually being re-colonized by both the Whiteman and others.

The founders of the African Union wanted a truly united Africa, but the result has been a club of cronies who talk, bark and nothing is done because of national sovereignty and neutrality. What Africa needs is an African Union of peoples and not states or a semblance of a unity of states; an African unity where all are Africans not citizens of countries where they really do not have any relation to it in their hearts, mind, attitudes, and no nationalist feelings. It is amazing that the Whiteman succeeded in Africa through the policy of divide and rule; this is well known and leaders of individual countries are still using the same policies successfully. A divided Africa can never develop. In spite of individual efforts, collectively and individually Africa is regressing two hundred years behind the rest of the world. Africa mocks itself by saying that Rome was not built in a day. Rome did not have any existing technology they could just replicate nor was it blessed with all the resources of Africa. It is even an insult to compare a country with a continent, but that is what Africa has been reduced to.

*The **emblem of the African Union** features a golden, boundary-less map of Africa inside two concentric circles, with stylised palm leaves shooting up on either side of the outer circle.*

1. *The palm leaves shooting up on either side of the outer circle stand for peace.*
2. *The gold circle again symbolizes Africa's wealth and bright future.*
3. *The green circle again stands for African hopes and aspirations.*
4. *The plain map of Africa without boundaries in the inner circle signifies African unity.*

The small interlocking red rings at base of the Emblem stand for African solidarity and the bloodshed for Liberation of Africa.

AU Anthem

> *1. Let us all unite and celebrate together*
> *The victories won for our liberation*
> *Let us dedicate ourselves to rise together*
> *To defend our liberty and unity*
>
> *2. O Sons and Daughters of Africa*
> *Flesh of the Sun and Flesh of the Sky*

Let us make Africa the Tree of Life

3. Let us all unite and sing together
To uphold the bonds that frame our destiny
Let us dedicate ourselves to fight together
For lasting peace and justice on earth

4. O Sons and Daughters of Africa
Flesh of the Sun and Flesh of the Sky
Let us make Africa the Tree of Life

5. Let us all unite and toil together
To give the best we have to Africa
The cradle of mankind and fount of culture
Our pride and hope at break of dawn.

6. O Sons and Daughters of Africa
Flesh of the Sun and Flesh of the Sky
Let us make Africa the Tree of Life

The Vision of the AU

- *The AU is Africa's premier institution and principal organization for the promotion of accelerated socio-economic integration of the continent, which will lead to greater unity and solidarity between African countries and peoples.*
- *The AU is based on the common vision of a united and strong Africa and on the need to build a partnership between governments and all segments of civil society, in particular women, youth and the private sector, in order to strengthen solidarity and cohesion amongst the peoples of Africa.*

As a continental organization it focuses on the promotion of peace, security and stability on the continent as a prerequisite for the implementation of the development and integration agenda of the Union.

The Objectives of the AU

- *To achieve greater unity and solidarity between the African countries and the peoples of Africa;*
- *To defend the sovereignty, territorial integrity and independence of its Member States;*
- *To accelerate the political and socio-economic integration of the continent;*
- *To promote and defend African common positions on issues of interest to the continent and its peoples;*
- *To encourage international cooperation, taking due account of the Charter of the United Nations and the Universal Declaration of Human Rights;*
- *To promote peace, security, and stability on the continent;*
- *To promote democratic principles and institutions, popular participation and good governance;*
- *To promote and protect human and peoples' rights in accordance with the African Charter on Human and Peoples' Rights and other relevant human rights instruments;*
- *To establish the necessary conditions which enable the continent to play its rightful role in the global economy and in international negotiations;*
- *To promote sustainable development at the economic, social and cultural levels as well as the integration of African economies;*
- *To promote co-operation in all fields of human activity to raise the living standards of African peoples;*
- *To coordinate and harmonize the policies between the existing and future Regional Economic Communities for the gradual attainment of the objectives of the Union;*

- *To advance the development of the continent by promoting research in all fields, in particular in science and technology;*
- *To work with relevant international partners in the eradication of preventable diseases and the promotion of good health on the continent.*

These are the African Union emblem, vision and objectives as culled from their web site. They are laudable, achievable, doable, and would propel Africa towards real independence and development. So what is the problem with achieving something so laudable and doable? The problem is that while all of these sound good on the paper on which it is written, the AU is a toothless dog without power or mandate to enforce the very objectives for which it was formed. So long as Africans want and need sovereign states, the AU is a waste of time, without the power it should have.

For Africa to develop at any pace to close the gap between developed and regressing economies it needs to quadruple its development rate. That cannot happen in an Africa with small and fragmented countries without the potential to do much on its own. Many people have suggested the strengthening of regional economic committees. But that is only for starts. Africa cannot develop without putting all its might and energy together. Africa needs a very strong AU and even stronger regional economic communities.

The advent of the African Union (AU) can be described as an event of great magnitude in the institutional evolution of the continent. On 9.9.1999, the Heads of States and Governments of the Organisation of African Unity issued a Declaration, (the Sirte Declaration) calling for the establishment of an African Union, with a view, inter alia, to accelerating the process of integration in the continent. The Declaration was to enable it play its rightful role in the global economy while addressing multifaceted social, economic and political problems compounded as they are by certain negative aspects of globalization.

The main objectives of the OAU were, inter alia, to rid the continent of the remaining vestiges of colonization and apartheid; to promote unity and solidarity among African States; to coordinate and intensify cooperation for development; to safeguard the sovereignty and territorial integrity of Member States and to promote international cooperation within the framework of the United Nations.

Indeed, as a continental organization the OAU provided an effective forum that enabled all Member States to adopt coordinated positions on matters of common concern to the continent in international fora and defended the interests of Africa effectively.

Through the OAU Coordinating Committee for the Liberation of Africa, the Continent worked and spoke as one with undivided determination in forging an international consensus in support of the liberation struggle and the fight against apartheid.

The Quest for Unity

African countries, in their quest for unity, economic and social development under the banner of the OAU, have taken various initiatives and made substantial progress in many areas which paved the way for the establishment of the AU. Noteworthy among these are:

- Lagos Plan of Action (LPA) and the Final Act of Lagos (FAL?) (1980); incorporating programmes and strategies for self-reliant development and cooperation among African countries.
- The African Charter on Human and People's Rights (Nairobi 1981) and the Grand Bay Declaration and Plan of Action on Human rights: two instruments adopted by the OAU to promote Human and People's Rights in the Continent. The Human Rights Charter led to the establishment of the African Human Rights Commission located in Banjul, The Gambia.

- Africa's Priority Programme for Economic recovery (APPER) - 1985: an emergency programme designed to address the development crisis of the 1980s, in the wake of protracted drought and famine that had engulfed the continent and the crippling effect of Africa's external indebtedness.
- OAU Declaration on the Political and Socio-Economic Situation in Africa and the Fundamental Changes taking place in the World (1990), which underscored Africa's resolve to take the imitative to determine its destiny and to address the challenges to peace, democracy and security.
- The Charter on Popular Participation adopted in 1990: a testimony to the renewed determination of the OAU to endeavour to place the African citizen at the centre of development and decision-making.
- The Treaty establishing the African Economic Community (AEC) - 1991: commonly known as the Abuja Treaty, it seeks to create the AEC through six stages culminating in an African Common Market using the Regional Economic Communities (RECs) as building blocks. The Treaty has been in operation since 1994.
- The Mechanism for Conflict Prevention, Management and Resolution (1993): a practical expression of the determination of the African leadership to find solutions to conflicts, promote peace, security and stability in Africa.
- Cairo Agenda for Action (1995): a programme for re-launching Africa's political, economic and social development.
- African Common Position on Africa's External Debt Crisis (1997): a strategy for addressing the Continent's External Debt Crisis.
- The Algiers decision on Unconstitutional Changes of Government (1999) and the Lome Declaration on the

framework for an OAU Response to Unconstitutional Changes (2000).

- The 2000 Solemn Declaration on the Conference on Security, Stability, Development and Cooperation: establishes the fundamental principles for the promotion of Democracy and Good Governance in the Continent.
- Responses to other challenges: Africa has initiated collective action through the OAU in the protection of environment, fighting international terrorism, combating the scourge of the HIV/AIDS pandemic, malaria and tuberculosis or dealing with humanitarian issues such as refugees and displaced persons, landmines, small and light weapons, among others.
- The Constitutive Act of the African Union: adopted in 2000 at the Lome Summit (Togo) entered into force in 2001.
- The New Partnership for Africa's Development (NEPAD): adopted as a Programme of the AU at the Lusaka Summit (2001).

The United States of Africa the way it was proposed by Gaddafi may not work.

However, a two digit per annum growth to enable Africa develop and stand to catch up with the rest of the world will not happen without a closer and more united Africa. If it were possible to repartition Africa, it would be necessary to return to the drawing board in terms of Socio-cultural relationships, religion, migration history, and language similarities. Doing this might end up having ten African countries instead of 53 and Africa would still be one. However, since no African country or Leader is willing to give up their Presidential title for the sake of the greater majority, Africa will remain fragments of small countries with the potential to propel itself and its people out of poverty if only it is determined to do so. Can the African Union be accorded more powers to enable it do the work and carry out the mission for which it was created? Many people ask how this is possible when the AU is not financially autonomous. There are many ways of making the AU autonomous. Besides subsidies from member states, the AU can become the supreme Land Lord of Africa and get all foreign companies dealing with Africa's natural resources and operating in Africa to pay taxes directly to the AU.

This way, the AU can mete out sanctions to countries that do not conform to the AU policies. This is not to say countries should increase taxes. Rather, as said elsewhere, taxes need to be reduced in order to provide the private sector with an enabling environment in which to do business. At the same time ways must be found to make the AU and RECs (Regional Economic Commissions) more autonomous and effective in carrying out their duties. The AU should as well be more involved in national elections and be able to veto those elections that are ravaged by fraud. The AU should be able to kick out non-conforming members and mete out sanctions to countries. But above all, it should be able to force countries to uphold their constitutions which should be the supreme instrument of any country. The AU could go as far as having a generalized constitution which will allow only for a few specific changes to be contextualized by individual countries or regions.

Africa Day

The first time I heard about *Africa Day,* which is May 25th was in Geneva. We celebrated it in pump and style at the global fund where I worked, while the AU ambassador to Switzerland organized a symposium on the theme "Africa's Development, Whose Responsibility?" The symposium which was celebrated in Geneva in 2009 was attended by many top international and African intellectuals. I heard some of the best brains from Africa speak. I heard business people, European heads of industry, the United Nations, the Swiss government, EU etc. Everyone agreed that as much as Africa could use external partners to develop, the responsibility for Africa's development rested with Africa and Africans. Africa has to decide if it wants to develop, how it wants to develop, who its partners should be, the nature of the partnership, how fast or how slow it wants to develop and then go on and do it rather than sit back and talk or wish it.

African countries celebrate independence days and international days, yet most Africans do not even know that there is an *Africa day* because it is neither talked about nor celebrated. This could be the one and truly biggest celebrated day all over Africa, with themes to showcase Africanism, origins, process, progress and goals besides African diversity and similarities. Celebrating an *Africa day* yearly will help restore pride in the African, foster peace and unity and highlight what the AU stands for, the common heritage and thus foster genuine cooperation, greater awareness and understanding of Africanism and propel Africa towards development.

The African Union can certainly pat itself on the back and show achievements which it has made over the years and those achievements are laudable, but they are just not enough to propel Africa towards real independence and development. Real independence is when Africans can choose who they want to lead them without foreign interference or interest, but those of Africans and the African state. The way the AU, African countries and the continent has been treated by their "partners", or "friends" or "colonial Masters" or super powers during the Libyan and Ivorian crises leave no doubt how powerless the AU is. Without its own army, relying on foreign armies owned by the people it is supposed to fight, how can the AU stand against such might? The AU looks like a big joke.

Africans have to make up their mind if they want to be really independent or if they want to be half independent or remain colonized. Africa is still chained to its colonial pasts and there is absolute need for one Africa, one language, one people with none feeling that they are superior to the other because of some features that they think are better than others. For this unity to be real and functional it might be best to shrink this continent into five or ten countries so that it can truly take the reins and develop.

CHAPTER 8

THE HISTORICAL IMPACT OF COLONIZATION AND MIGRATION ON AFRICA

Melissa Snell says:

> "The study of medieval African societies has value, not only because we can learn from all civilizations in all time frames, but because these societies reflected and influenced a myriad of cultures that, due to the Diaspora that began in the 16th century, have spread throughout the modern world."

Thus according to Melissa, the study of African history is relevant to modern day society, not only to Africans.

The easiest way to understand African history is to divide it into phases. The phases are as follows:

Pre-Colonial Africa

During this era, two major movements influenced Africa: the expansion and consolidation of Islam and the dispersion of the Bantu peoples which led to the development of many kingdoms and empires. [7] At this time too, Muslim traders from North Africa shipped goods across the Sahara using large camel caravans -- on average around a thousand camels although there's a record which mentions caravans travelling between Egypt and Sudan that had 12,000 camels.

---

[7] Wikipedia

These caravans brought in mainly luxury goods such as textiles, silks, beads, ceramics, ornamental weapons, and utensils. These were traded for gold, ivory, woods such as ebony, and agricultural products such as kola nuts (which is a stimulant containing caffeine). They also brought their religion, Islam, which spread along the trade routes. Nomads living in the Sahara traded salt, meat and their knowledge in exchange for cloth, gold, cereal, and slaves[8]

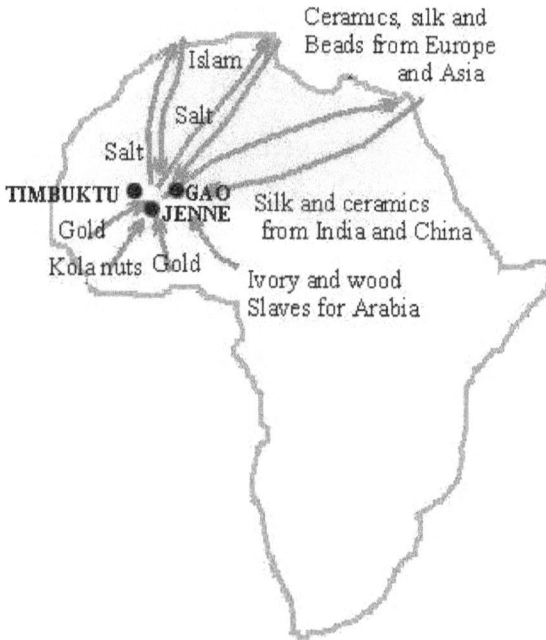

About twenty Kingdoms existed in precolonial Africa and had recognized systems of leadership and self rule. History books recognize the following amongst others

- The Kingdom of Mali or The Songhai Empire ruled by Sonni Ali.

Alistair Boddy-Evans calls Timbuktu, one of the centres of the Songhai Empire, **the Eldorado of Africa.** The other

---

[8] Wikipedia

centres of this empire were Mali and Jenne which were major trading centres. Today these are three, small, separate countries.

- The Ghanaian or Ashanti empire: The Wikipedia has it that"The **Ghana Empire** that flourished from 750 to 1076 AD was one of the most prominent empires of Western Africa in the ancient times. The Ghana Empire covered an area that spread from Mauritania to Senegal, including the western parts of Mali. The Ghana Empire became rich by trading in salt and gold. It is interesting to note that the ancient empire of Ghana was in no ways related to modern Ghana. The entire stretch of the **Ghana Empire** was 500 miles away from modern-day Ghana. The earliest settlers of Ghana Empire belonged to the Soninke clan. At the centre of prosperity of the Ghana Empire was the trade and commerce that flourished on the basis of the gold reserve of the empire. The mixed economy of Ghana Empire consisted of extensive agriculture, carpentry, pottery, iron smelting, gold smiting and cloth manufacturing. The main goods traded were salt, copper, gold and slaves.[9]
- The Yuroba Kingdom: The Yoruba People, of whom there are more than twenty-five million, occupy the south-western corner of Nigeria along the Dahomey border and extends into Dahomey itself. To the east and north the Yoruba culture reaches its approximate limits in the region of the Niger River. However, ancestral cultures directly related to the Yoruba once flourished well north of the Niger. Portuguese explorers "discovered" the Yoruba cities and kingdoms in the fifteenth century, but cities such as Ife and Benin, among others, had been standing at their present sites for at least five hundred years before the European

[9] Wikipédia

arrival. Archaeological evidence indicates that a technologically and artistically advanced, proto-Yoruba (Nok), were living somewhat north of the Niger in the first millennium B.C., and they were then already working with iron. Ife was the first of all Yoruba cities. Oyo and Benin came later and expanded because of their strategic locations at a time when trading became prosperous.[10]

- The Igbo Kingdom. It is believed that the Igbo originated in an area about 100 miles north of their current location at the confluence of the Niger and Benue Rivers. They share linguistic ties with their neighbours the Bini, Igala, Yoruba, and Idoma, with the split between them probably occurring between five and six thousand years ago. The first Igbo in the region may have moved onto the Awka-Orlu plateau between four and five thousand years ago, before the emergence of sedentary agricultural practices. As this early group expanded, so too did the Igbo kingdom. The earliest surviving Igbo art forms are from the 10th century (Igbo Ukwu) and the fine quality of those copper alloy castings suggest that Igbo society had already achieved a level of technology rivalling contemporary Europeans.[11]

- The Zulu Kingdom: The **Zulu Kingdom** was a monarchy in Southern Africa that extended along the coast of the Indian Ocean from the Tugela River in the south to Pongola River in the north.

The small kingdom grew to dominate much of what is today KwaZulu-Natal in Southern Africa, but when it came into conflict with the British Empire in the 1870s during the Anglo-Zulu War, it was defeated despite an early Zulu victory in the war. The area was subsequently absorbed into

---

[10] Wikipédia
[11] Wikipédia

the Colony of Natal and later became part of the Union of South Africa.[12]

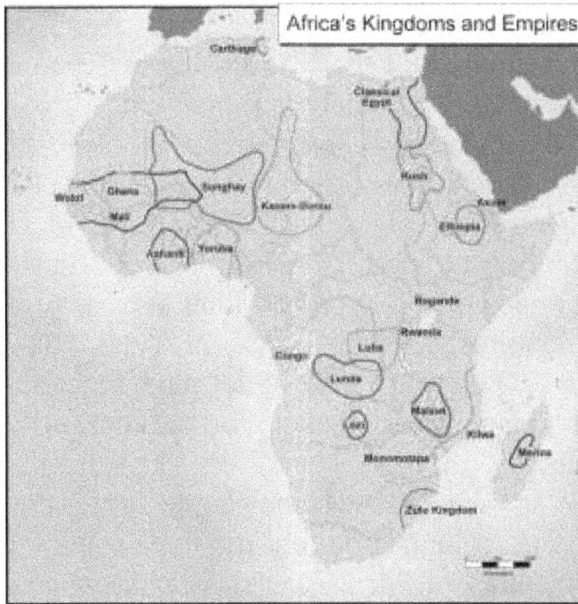

Africa's Kingdoms and Empires

The kingdoms of Africa do not make up to twenty two kingdoms. Fifty four countries in Africa with the divide and rule influence of the colonial past is a deliberate effort by the masters to keep Africa underdeveloped. Further more, most African kingdoms originated or had ties with the Niger river. Africa can come together to develop itself.

Colonial Africa and Post colonial Africa

Colonial Africa is a long period of ancient colonization with the Arabs from the North, through early colonization and the scramble for and partition of Africa by Europeans, which is where the problems of Africa as it is now can safely be said began.

Aidan Southall in his article "state formation in Africa" says that:

---

[12] Wikipédia

"Africa is tremendously important in the recent study of the state, not only because more new states were formed in Africa during the 1960s than had been formed in the rest of the world for many centuries, but also because immediately pre-colonial Africa, at the end of the nineteenth and beginning of the twentieth century, offered more examples of emergent states than any other region of the world. This was because in other continents such as Asia or Europe most of the smaller states of this type had long been absorbed into larger empires....Thus Africa provides the largest number of examples both of recent indigenous states and of contemporary states formed out of colonial territories.

Africans are one and the same people but for the impact of migration and colonization on the continent. The first recorded colonization of Africa dates as far back as 570-526 BC, with the invasion of Greece into Egypt for economic purposes. During that period a Greek mercantile colony was established at Naucratis, some fifty miles from the present day Alexandria. Down the centuries, the colonization of Africa, the migration and expansion of both external and internal forces can be attributed to the following:

Economic Reasons

From the 7th century, Arab trade with sub-Saharan Africa gradually led to the colonization of certain parts of east Africa, especially around the Zanzibar. North Africa especially Morocco, also attempted to conquer some parts of Africa in the Sahel area but it was not successful. Nonetheless, through trading with these countries, Arab influence and interest remained in those parts. The Arabs came on camel and horse back and so colonized the Northern part of Africa and small pockets of the rest of Africa while the Europeans came through the sea and colonized the coastal parts of Africa.

According to Vincent Khapoya, European expansion into Africa for economic reasons started as far back as 332 BC, when Alexander the Great was welcomed as a liberator in the Persian-occupied Egypt. The focus of this discourse is, however the late 18th to 19th centuries when there was a scramble for Africa by France, Britain, Spain and Portugal.

As Khapoya discusses, all colonial powers exercised significant attention to the economies of the situation. This included the acquisition of land, enforced labour, introduction of cash crops, even to the neglect of food crops, halting inter-African trading patterns of pre-colonial times, introduction of labourers from India, and the continuation of Africa as a source of raw materials for European industry, therefore a continent not to be industrialized.[13] The search for raw materials and markets to sell surplus products made expansion and colonization a necessity for the foreign powers.

Adventure

Europeans, in a bid to find other continents which in historical parlance was called the Dark Continent, set out simply for adventure and when they found what they described as unconquered territory, they claimed it for their various countries. The assumption in the adventurers' minds seems to be that their home country or known territory alone was recognized and those unknown had to be owned by simply visiting or finding them! This self-centred and simplistic stance is what led to the "discovery" of other lands and peoples. In the case of Africa, after coming in friendship and being welcomed by fragmented chieftaincies and kingdoms, the adventurer birthed slavery.

Slavery

African history can never be told without including the slave trade which started from the North by Arabs and spread

---

[13] Wikipédia

to the rest of the continents when Europeans and the Americans came in. The bleak irony is that rather than earning him respect, the sheer strength of the African people caused the African to be carted off for forced labour in foreign countries. There he received most inhuman treatment and was not recognized as a human being at all, especially because he was black. Most colonial masters colonized Africans as if the colour of their brains was supposed to be the same as the colour of their skin or as if the blood that flowed through their veins was black, not red.

Religion

From the North the Arabs came with their Muslim religion to convert the colonies. For, although the colonies believed in a God, the God they worshiped was a nameless god and since the gods were as diverse as the people they met, Islam was introduced or imposed and more souls gained for Mohamed. The Europeans and the Americans, however, came with the Bible in one hand through the sea to talk about a Christian GOD who had sent his only begotten son to come and save the savages they met who worshiped idols because they knew there was a higher being who created them even though they did not know who that Being was.

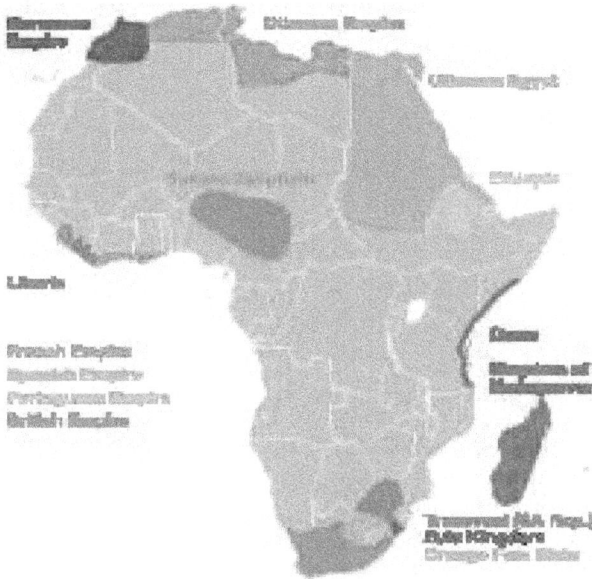

Map of African continent circa 1850s

From "the late 19th century, European imperial powers engaged in a major territorial scramble and occupied most of the continent, creating many colonial territories, and leaving only two fully independent states: Ethiopia (known to Europeans as "Abyssinia"), and Liberia. Egypt and Sudan were never formally incorporated into any European colonial empire. However, after the British occupation of 1882, Egypt was effectively under British administration until 1922"[14]

Britain, France, Belgium, Germany and Portugal colonized Africa and after the Second World War when decolonization began the effects of the administrative styles of these countries on their colonies impacted the countries and continue to do so to date. The division of Africa was made with the sole interest of the colonial masters. Neither culture,

---

[14] Wikipédia

- 131 -

or natural boundaries nor existing relationships were taken into consideration. This has given rise to the fragmentation and artificial boundaries in Africa, which greatly impedes its development.

According to Khapoya "The French, the Portuguese, the Germans and the Belgians exercised a highly centralized type of administration called "direct rule" while the British on the other hand, sought to rule by identifying local power holders and encouraging or forcing these to administer for the British Empire. This was indirect rule.

France ruled from France, appointing chiefs, individuals without considering traditional criteria, but rather loyalty to France. France established two large colonial federations in Africa, French West Africa and French Equatorial Africa. It appointed officials, passed laws and had to approve any measures passed by colonial assemblies.

These colonial boundaries and administrative styles have been inherited by African countries who are supposed to develop their own administrative styles that will be country specific and context applied. The situation is compounded by the fact that the colonial masters imposed their culture and language on the different territories and Africa, which formally had close cultural and linguistic identities, found itself with diverse foreign languages and cultures to add to its own languages dialects and habits. Along the way, a lot got lost and now Africa needs to plough its way back to understand where it came from, who its people are and where they want to go and their need to get there together.

Culture

Nowhere has Africa suffered more the effects of migration and colonization than in its culture. Today there is hardly an African culture because years of colonization, migration and suppression of what the colonial masters thought was not good was discouraged and eventually abandoned by Africans. It is painful to think that archaeologists have unearthed artworks in Africa which predates civilization elsewhere, but that when the colonial masters came, (Arabians, Europeans or Americans) the story of deculturisation was effected consistently and throughout Africa. They made Africans believe that everything African was bad. The idea was: give up what you produce because what we have is cheaper and better than yours. Without thought or arguments, African forefathers abandoned their culture of art, music, dance, sports and religion. African cultural renaissance movements are trying to find and bring back African culture from documents and stories told by colonial masters'

Languages

Africa is the most multilingual continent in the world, and it is not rare for individuals to fluently speak not only multiple African languages, but one or more European ones as well. There are four major language families indigenous to Africa. The Afro-Asiatic languages are a language family of about 240 languages spoken by some 285 million people throughout the Horn of Africa, North Africa, the Sahel, and Southwest Asia.

- The Nilo-Saharan language family consists of more than a hundred languages spoken by 30 million people. Nilo-Saharan languages are spoken by tribes in Chad, Ethiopia, Kenya, Sudan, South Sudan, Uganda, and Northern Tanzania.
- The Niger–Congo language family covers much of Sub-Saharan Africa and is probably the largest language family in the world in terms of different languages.
- The Khoisan languages number about fifty and are spoken in Southern Africa by approximately 120,000 people. Many of the Khoisan languages are endangered. The Khoi and San peoples are

considered the original inhabitants of this part of Africa[15].

The linguistic ancestry of Africa shows only four countries. How developed those four countries would have been instead of the current fifty four, which only make Africa and Africans underdeveloped.

Following the end of colonialism, nearly all African countries adopted official languages that originated outside the continent, although several countries also granted legal recognition to indigenous languages.

In numerous countries, English and French are used for communication in the public spheres of government, commerce, and education. Arabic, Portuguese, Afrikaans and Spanish are examples of languages that trace their origin to outside of Africa, and that are used by millions of Africans today, both in the public and private spheres. Italian is spoken by some in former Italian colonies in Africa. German is spoken in Namibia, which was a German protectorate.

It does not matter from what perspective one looks at the African continent. From its religious beliefs, through its cultural past to its linguistic ancestry, without colonial intervention and occupation, there would not have been at any one time more than six countries in Africa. Had imperial transgression not taken place, Africa would be a stronger and more united continent, poised to develop or already developed. However, while each of the fifty-five American states is bigger than some African countries, Africa is continually fragmenting and dividing instead of uniting to make development easier. When Europeans are uniting to the extent of being their brothers' keepers and pulling lagging economies up, Africa is splitting and creating more countries. The administrative styles of the colonial masters which African countries continued with have helped to kill development.

The United Arab Emirates (UAE)

Dubai and all the United Arab Emirates (UAE) countries are among the most beautiful of the developed world, a marvel at what they have turned a desert into. And yet Chiek Zayed who founded the UAE from the richest emirate Abu Dhabi modelled the UAE on Libya. A visionary, he realized that they had so much oil wealth. He could not understand why any citizen should live in the hills and in poverty. At the same time he understood the strength of numbers. So he went to his other neighbours and proposed a union. Bahrain and one other small country refused but the others accepted; so they formed the UAE. They built houses for all their citizens, redistributing the oil wealth, called them from the desert and gave each a hundred and fifty thousand US dollars to furnish their houses. Those who wanted to work were trained in the appropriate skills. The UEA are the only countries in the world where the nationals make five or six times the salary of an expatriate. The population of foreigners is seven times that of nationals and nationals do not do menial jobs. They are proud to be in their countries and live well.

The UAE makes Europe look like a kitchen because all they had to do was copy and paste and perfected or improved what they were copying. It is no wonder then that the UAE has the only two seven-star hotels in the whole world. Why could Africa not do something similar, unless it is contented with its little countries which on their own can never hope to develop but whose resources, if pulled together, could make Africa the giant of the world?

Trading within Africa

In personal sales, the taste of the pudding is in the eating. That is why most products sold through representatives like Avon, Mary Kay, GNLD, Tianchi etc., the consultant has to be using the product because the best way to advertise the product is to use it yourself. Africa in and of itself is a huge market; if it produced most of the products it used that would propel it towards development. But Africa is more of a consumer continent than a producing one. If Africa wanted to consume its own products, it would not have them. It relies on the importation of basic goods like rice and salt for survival. If the African Union were to use its economies of scale by producing most of its basic goods, huge industries would be constructed across the continent, which would not only create employment at various levels but provide the goods and services needed at a cheaper cost.

The South with its rich soil and opportunities can become the bread basket of food for Africa while the arid north concentrates on cereals. Production will be increased in each region and each will only need to buy what they need from each other. This will not mean ignoring the rest of the world. Rather, it will mean improving products by specializing and producing what the various regions of the African environment is best and making sure that goods and services can compete in the world market.

"What better gift can a man get than constructing the future of his country?" Alejandro Toledo - Peruvian President (2006).

"The Mind that practices Racism and Segregation is the primitive and most Primitive Mind. It functions adversely to the Contemporary and most Evolved Mind that shuns these concepts" Who then is Emancipated, You or I? Terry Yong Yuh

CHAPTER 9

COMMUNICATION AND INFORMATION, LESSONS LEARNED AND SHARED

A little mix up in communication can yield grave disaster. For example, the cattle owner herded his cattle to drink in the only stream during the dry season and while the herd of cattle was drinking, a villager came by and said angrily,

"The cows should not be drinking water from the river, they are dirtying the water and you are trespassing". The cattle owner said, "I will be gone as soon as the cattle finish, then the water will be clean in a little while"

"But while the cattle was drinking the water, the people downstream could not fetch water to drink"

"What do you want me to do, my brother?" asked the cattle owner who was Fulani.

"Your brother?" asked the villager, "Do I look like you? How dare you call me your brother?"

"Na just way for talk na Masa?" the Fulani man responded

Later on, the villager went and reported to anyone who could listen that the Fulani had not only trespassed through their land, but were now claiming to own the river. Before long all the youths had gathered in the square with knives, clubs and den guns. What ensured was a war which left many dead. Men, cattle and property lost for nothing. In the end when you asked what provoked the war, no one could say accurately what had transpired. Many wars are provoked and fought through miscommunication and lack of communication.

The human being is a communicating animal. Everything in life communicates in one way or the other. The English have it that you dress as you want to be addressed. Dressing therefore speaks a lot. A person in a casual wear says I want to be relaxed. This occasion should not be formal, or depending on the circumstances, it can mean I don't care about the occasion or the person who invited me. Nelson Mandela made the printed African shirts "a la mode" when he started wearing them. A woman in a short sexy dress says see my beauty, my assets; don't think about my brain while a woman in a suit transmits the message, this is business, its formal and no-nonsense; I want to be taken seriously, think about my brains, not my legs or my butts. The accessories for a man or woman also have their own message to communicate. Is the hand bag, wrist watch, shoes or tie designer or not? What is the price tag? That tells an observant person what you are all about because the packaging too for a person is important and does communicate.

Dressing also depends on the season and the location in the world. I remember as a young girl, I ordered things from "Springle" catalogues in London. I ordered cloths including boots while I lived in Victoria the hot coastal town of Cameroon. I wore them too and felt not only on top of the world but in fashion. Then I went to study in the US and discovered to my consternation that the booths were meant for winter to ward off cold and not for dressing. The way you wear your hair, up or down, braided, natural or straightened suggests the way you want to be seen and how you want to be taken. I let my hair down long and loose these days even for job interviews because I am at that age where I either know what I am supposed to know or I don't so I don't care. However, because of my business background and the types of jobs I am likely to interview for, I will wear a suit to any job interview because that is the culture of my profession. People in marketing have to look flashy while those in communication have to dress casual or formal depending on what the assignment is.

Where you want to go also determines your mode of dressing, which also makes a statement. Are you going walking, strolling or going for a picnic? When a woman wears high-hilled shoes or stilettos to a garden function or picnic, it is obvious she does not know what she is doing but wants people to believe that she knows how to dress. The occasion or type of function determines what kind of dress code is required; formal, informal or traditional. The new generation of African children dresses what they see on the screen, not understanding that what they see on the screen is not what people necessarily wear on the street. So, as Africans if we are embracing a culture, we should embrace it well.

Office space and furniture, although inanimate, communicate. When people enter an office, the size of the offices and the type of furniture tell who the boss is and the rank of the various employees. The distance between the offices, also makes a statement. When a guest enters an office or house, the manner in which they are received or sent off communicates either the importance of the person or the relationship between the guest and the host. It is not everyone you stand up to greet or see to the door. All of these communicate. Even the chairs or their position of sitting communicate.

A person's car communicates something about the person, the colour of the car also communicates; are they loud, flashy, gentle, discreet or what? Thus, because the human being is basically a communicating being, and everything around us communicates, what we say is never a problem but the way we say it, and the circumstances under which we say it makes an enormous difference. The human being communicates verbally and non-verbally. The tone of voice, volume, emotion, rhythm, posture and body language, all communicate, and depending on the listeners' circumstances, the interpretation and meaning of the communication is filtered; they understand what they want and react accordingly.

Most conflicts are as a result of miscommunication, lack of accurate information, misinterpretation or just the perception of being snubbed, insulted or ignored. A conflict that generates into violence, war and the loss of lives can just be a matter of how something which happened or was even thought to have happened was reported. The circumstances and environment too have their own place in determining the context and how the message is interpreted.

I attended a meeting with a civil rights activist and as we moved along, we discussed our current problems and for most Anglophone Cameroonians, it is the Anglophone problem or the perception of one and he said "the SCNC (Southern Cameroons National Council) is Biya's creation" "What" I answered "No, it cannot be, I was there in Buea at 'the All Anglophone Conference' AAC 1 and in Bamenda for AAC 2".

Quietly he asked "What were the conferences all about?"

"To discuss the Anglophone problems or perception of problems with the head of State"

"So what was the outcome? Were we ever listened to?"

"No" I answered.

"So you see, the SCNC is Biya's creation because at the beginning all we were asking for was dialogue, but our peaceful requests were met with water cannons and tear gas, so is there any reason why from just defending a people's right to free expression the conference turned to demands for separation and then secession?"

I had never really thought about it in those terms but he rested his case and we went our separate ways.

MEDIA

Communication has been called the fourth estate and in many countries has brought down governments. All the tools of communication can also be used in Africa to build or destroy Africa. We thank GOD that in many communities, there are community radios which broadcast in the language of that community. There can no longer be the excuse of ignorance or lack of information as the reason for failure. The community radios can be used as propaganda machines to build Africa by talking about its roots and the inter-relationship of its regions.

While the fourth estate is strong and vocal in most developed countries, the media in most African countries has a semblance of "Freedom of press" while in reality it is weak, mostly state owned and controlled. Those who try to say anything anti-government are shut down; journalists are locked up, some killed (in the eighties, Dela Giwa was killed in Nigeria by a letter bomb). The fourth estate, which in most countries has brought down politicians by exposing the ills inherent in their administration, in Africa is afraid to lift up its head for fear of being locked up or worse.

Whether we like it or not, Africa needs a truly free media and those who go out in search of news and journalists who are willing to put themselves in the frontline of the fight. Africans, individually and collectively, need to make up their minds to be the architects of the change, the progress and the development and the progress decidedly needed.

When CNN, BBC, France, Africa 24 and most TV or radio stations report about events in Africa, there is a lack of *Africanness* in their perspective. There is need for an African media to report issues from Africa, by Africans, giving the world an African perspective. All the recent events that happened in Tunisia, Egypt, Ivory Coast, Libya and elsewhere in Africa have been reported from all these media houses that are not African and do not have African interest at heart. Things happening in the African backyards are given back to

Africa from foreign perspectives. It is not usually lies that are reported but the truth according to the others' perspectives.

a. Community Radio

Community radio and vernacular was used to incite violence in Rwanda. It can also be used to foster love, cooperation, fight racism, tribalism; it can be used to educate the grassroots and the national population. Community radios can become huge tools for diffusing messages to the population. Because everyone understands some language, these radio stations can be used to educate anyone on any subject from history to democracy. Just recruiting young graduates who can talk well in the various vernaculars and giving them topics to discuss over the radio at various times may well be able to propel rural areas into development and out of poverty.

b. The Cost of Communication

The mobile phone and social networks have also reached the African continent. However, because Africa depends on other peoples satellites communication within Africa and to Africa is still, ironically, very expensive. A ten dollar card to call the United States from Europe would give 420 minutes of air time while the same card to call Africa will barely give you 60 minutes. And so, in spite of Africa's poverty it still pays very expensively for most basic services. If only Africa would come together and work as one towards its development.

Development and the Private Sector

Every country needs a government to make policies, protect the citizens, and provide justice and orientation. However, in most African countries every child seems to go to school with the notion that they can come out and work with the government because the government provides security. True, most governments provide security because they will pay you whether you deliver or not. That is exactly what is wrong with most African countries and that is what delays development.

A look at the World Bank doing business statistics for 2010 shows a direct correlation between the level of development of a country and the ranking of ease of doing business. The more difficult the business environment is the less developed a country, thus reemphasizing the relationship between development and the private sector. Development cannot take place without policies in place to enable the private sector to thrive.

No government can provide jobs for all its citizens, so what African governments need are strong civil services, which are highly paid, with specific mandates to deliver and an even stronger private sector. Private sector, national or foreign to help develop a country cannot and will not happen without an enabling environment.

The private sectors' main objectives are profit making for its shareholders. However, this is not exclusive of development or social responsibilities because studies show that the more developed a people the more disposable income they will have to spend, thus the more money a company will make for its shareholders. What do African countries need to do to attract investors, improve its private sector and therefore the livelihood of its citizens?

First, back to education, governments should provide competitive services with the right skills at affordable prices as the Asians have done. They should reduce the cost of doing business by providing incentives for companies to come and invest. Reduce and simplify taxes in such a way as to make tax evasion unnecessary.

Governments should also provide education to all persons applying to do business where the simple rudiments of planning, management, accounting and taxation will be taught so that both formal and informal sectors understand the different taxes and why they have to pay what and where they need to do so. In Cameroon, for example, and in some African countries, the state makes a budget and never realizes what it is supposed to get, not because the money is not there or the business people are not paying in taxes but because innocent business people are being duped by tax officers and most of the money that should go into the state coffers ends up in private pockets and while the state is poor, there are individuals who are sitting rich.

If the private sector is given the respect and the recognition it deserves, no one in the private sector needs to envy those in the public sector because of the perceived power and rights which they have as civil servants. All sectors work collectively for the development of the country and each is not only important but necessary to the development and harmony of the whole.

In any given country in Africa, the informal sector is bigger than the formal sector because of the difficulties in setting up businesses and the capital requirements for big businesses. On the same level, although joint ventures would solve a lot of Africa's private sectors woes, joint ventures do not succeed very well because Africans refuse to respect the norms of joint ventures. When an individual has an idea and is looking for shareholders, they make promises which they forget as soon as the business takes off. They start looking at the business as if it were a sole proprietorship and start refusing to share information, data and dividends to shareholders.

Joint ventures are on the rise as global companies increasingly expand into emerging economies. They offer great benefits, but finding a suitable local partner in Africa to venture with can be difficult says *TradeInvestAfrica*. As growth opportunities diminish in domestic markets, companies in developed countries are increasingly shifting their attention to Africa and other emerging economies, which are touted as the markets of the future. According to management consultant McKinsey & Co, Africa currently offers the highest rates of return in the developing world and companies that enter the continent early will have great opportunities to create markets, establish brands and long-term relationships.[15]

The perception that most African countries are corrupt and not trustworthy to do business with means that most foreign companies venturing into Africa see the benefits of joint ventures but have to look carefully before they partner with any African company. This makes joint ventures sometimes difficult because finding the right local partner can mean the difference between success and failure. African countries therefore have to put strong laws in place to protect both national and foreign partners in a joint venture. This needs to change at the legislative level and at policy levels too. Talk of a mental revolution? We need it in all aspects of life in Africa in order to play catch up or even be developed to any level; a level where the basic needs of every citizen are met to a certain extent.

The private sector too, with all good policies in place, cannot thrive if the policies are written on paper but are never implemented. Again, the private sector will not thrive without the necessary skills needed to work in the private sector. Managers are certainly needed. Yet it is the technicians who produce the products which need to be marketed. America came up with AGOA (African Growth and Opportunity Act) in a bid to ease trade between African countries and America. However, the level of exploitation of this tool is very low because not many African countries can and do meet the quality standards which America imposes on its imports. Why is that so? Answer: because the African countries have no quality standards, not to talk of those which can be enforced. If they exist, they are not enforced and enforcement has to face corruption. The selfish non-partisan questions arise: What would happen to poor quality and shoddy materials? What

---

[15] Nelly Nyagah

would happen to making the most gain at the least cost? What will happen to the lack-lustre concept of just getting by instead of thriving?

Public Private Partnerships: The way forward?

At the Global Fund to fight against HIV/AIDS, tuberculosis and malaria, there was increased talk about Public Private Partnerships (PPP) as if it was a newly invented concept. Are PPPs a new concept or an old concept just redefined or realigned? Is it not business as usual in an unusual way? Are PPPs therefore the way forward for Africa's development?

Most governments would like to be able to make life easier and better for their citizens, but because they do not have all the resources needed in the quantities required to do so, they need to partner with the private sector. Collectively, the private sector can be richer than the state and have better opportunities than the state. So in order for the state to partner with the private sector in a win-win situation, the government needs to identify its priority areas, ask the private sector to bid for the contracts and do it with the government on a cost sharing manner for the investment and the returns on investments.

If the government needs to build roads for example, it cannot afford to do it on its own resources, so it can look for private external or internal partners who would construct the road according to pre-agreed standards, then collect the tolls for an agreed period of time after which they hand over the road to the government. The same thing can go for many social or basic projects.

Military

Nothing has expanded in most Sub Saharan African countries like the military since independence. With frequent coups, wars, territorial quarrels and dictators needing protection, nothing else has witnessed such expenditure as the army. The military budget for most countries is higher than that for health, education and other basics. War is never an option for any country, for one reason, it is costly, and then rebuilding a country after a war usually takes longer than the war took. And these are only part of the grim gains of war. Prevention can be covered since there are usually signs in a country which any discerning person can see that could lead to war; when such signs are evident, measures should be taken to prevent the situation from degenerating into war.

Financial Institutions

The boy was in primary school when his parents died in a ghastly road accident. He was the third of six children, two boys and four girls. Someone had to drop out of school to try to feed the family. Being the elder boy he gallantly opted to do so. He did petty businesses, opened a road-side stand where he sold cigarettes and call cards. Then he had a brilliant business idea and someone advised him to go and open an account in one of the new micro finance institutions that had started in the neighbourhood. He did so and every day the Bank sent one of their tellers to collect his savings and take to the Bank. After six months, he had qualified for a loan and the micro finance institution was ready to give him a loan if he first of all deposited a caution. He deposited the caution, bribed the bank manager and got a small loan to increase his business. Then he realized that he really was not making much profit because the interest on the loan was too much. So he borrowed money from friends to repay the loan and get his caution back or so he thought. After he repaid the loan, the Bank said he could not get his caution because all the money he was supposed to have saved had not been deposited in the bank. The poor young man tried to understand all the grammar the Bank Manger was telling him to no avail. All he knew was that he had been tricked out of his money and now he owed other people plus his sister who would not be able to go to school. He spent many weeks going to and from the Bank and one day he got there to realize that the door was locked and the micro finance institution had closed.

For development to take place there must be enough money in circulation to permit the Private Sector to thrive. As has been stressed, a strong and vibrant Private Sector is the route to fast and sustainable development. However, most African countries have weak financial systems, difficult conditions and access to credit. The notion here is not to give loans without security to companies and individuals. There is a need for there to be a balance between the availability of credit, access to credit, good projects to fund and ease of repayment of the loans in order to enable the institutions to continue to function and serve everyone. For this to happen, the state needs to put policies in place which protect both financial institutions' interests to make a profit, and the customers' interests. Policies need to be enacted to ease access to credit and also swiftly penalize defaulters. What this means is that the judicial system should be such that everyone, nationals, foreigners, individuals and institutions feel protected. And, of course, the judicial system should be the same for everyone, irrespective of social standing.

There isn't going to be a one size fits all solution or even a quick fix for our financial institutions. But every country needs to uphold some minimum international and continental standards reinforced by its national money and customs. No one or group of individuals should be allowed to open any financial institution, collect money from both investors and customers, mismanage it and then disappear with equanimity. At the worst, there should be national laws monitoring the time a person with a complete application file puts it in a Bank and the time it takes for the file to be treated and the loan disbursed. Many Banks fail for a number of reasons but the most rampant is the corrupt practice of kickbacks which weakens the customers' business venture and their ability and willingness to repay the loan. "After all" the customer reasons, "I didn't get all the money I wanted and I shared what I got with the Bank employee so why should I be obliged to repay the loan alone?" Bankers need to know that they, as much as every business person, are there to carter for the needs of the clients and not to get fat on the sweat of their clients and to the detriment of their employers.

It has gone down the records that "Africans work for Africa as if they are working for someone else". Africa needs to change the master-slave mentality and replace it with me, mine, us, our country and continent mentality.

Examples abound where in good faith, foreign financial institutions come with money to help foster development in a country, with conditions that the loans be given out to groups who will use the loans, repay it and it would become a revolving fund where others could continue to profit from. Smart people quickly form the groups, collect the money, share it and within a short time, the group dis- integrates, the money is never repaid, some members die and what was supposed to be a good initiative is killed.

The way forward: the time is now

During the 2010 World Cup played in Africa for the very first time, the theme song was wittingly "The time is now". Yes, Africa's time to develop is now or it would take another fifty years for development to happen.

The development of Sub Saharan Africa is the responsibility of Africa. Africa, fifty years after independence, has certainly moved forward in many areas relevant to development: Education, Agriculture, infrastructure etc. The pace of development for people who just need to copy and paste is slow and at the rate it is going it will never catch up nor close the gap. Africa needs political will and a commitment to develop; otherwise development for Sub Saharan Africa would only be talk and wishful thinking.

To achieve even half of its potentials, Africa needs a mental revolution, a revolution of people who do not only follow but think and act; an intellectual mind-set that thinks of the whole rather than the individual countries and regions. Intellectuals who are not intellectuals in name but people whose work, whose thesis, whose attitudes and careers add value to the continent and also to their existence. On another note the educational systems left in place by colonial masters have to be overhauled to reflect the needs of the continent. Africa's educational systems have to be focused on the skills needed to propel Africa to development. More technical schools at all levels need to be built. Specialized schools based on identified natural resources of each region should be constructed so that our natural resources can compete in the global market.

Africa needs to go back to the drawing board, revisit some historical facts and use them to design its path to development. Africans have to understand that Africa is too divided to develop. There is therefore need for it to come together and strengthen its ties through the common heritage binding it. Africans all came from similar roots and have a similar background. Most African migration started from around the river Niger and moved outwards. Migration has influenced changes in culture, languages and lifestyles, but it does not change the fact that the origin is the same. If this theory is pushed far, one can say that man as a whole has one origin. If the others have understood and are fighting to unite so that they can use their numerical strength and comparative advantages for each other's good then Africa can do the same. After all Michael Moore said, *"When we see a good idea from another country, we grab it. Cars, wine:"*

Someone made a statement that Africans are working for Africa as if they are working for someone else. What this means is that Africans still have a colonized mentality and so works for the continent without love or dedication. This can be perceptible in the many areas where Africans excel outside the continent, but when they come home the output is not the same. This is peculiar for example with Africa's professional footballers, medical doctors etc. The argument is always that the circumstances and environment is different. This may be true, but what they are really saying is that they prefer to enjoy the facilities which other nations and continents have built. How would Africa be built too and how would it attain the standards others have set if all hands are not put on deck? Africans have to make the conscious decision to unite; to come together and work to decolonize its mentalities and break the yoke which still ties it to its colonial past. Africa has to decide to stand up like a mature continent and be counted amongst its peers. Africa therefore must become truly independent in a globalized world. In a globalized world Africa needs to own its own satellite in order to use it for its own information and technological advancements. With this, it would decrease its costs of communication, develop its social networking and have a niche that is uniquely African.

Africa cannot stand alone in a globalized world. It needs partners to help it develop. However, if Africa does not understand that there are no friends in a globalized world and no free lunches; If Africa opens its arms and doors foolishly to these new "friends" coming to help propel it towards development then one day Africa would wake up and someone would have the title deed to the continent and it may just have cost him/her two cents.

There is strength in unity and when the centre breaks, things fall apart and the result is chaos. Therefore Africa's route to development can be facilitated by a stronger African Union (AU) which is the supreme Landlord of Africa and which can be financed through resource extraction fees, providing it the independence to carry out activities to help propel Africa in development. An African Union which will supervise elections and be able to mete out sanctions to countries which deserve to be sanctioned; an African Union which is truly what the founding fathers fought for and intended to put in place; an African Union that will cause *Africa day* to be celebrated throughout Africa; a celebration of what Africa is and how it wants the world to recognize it,

Beatrice Fri Bime

strong and united and with regional bodies; a strong Africa that is respected and counted amongst its peers.

Margaret Mead said *"Never doubt that a small group of thoughtful citizens can change the world. Indeed, it is the only thing that ever has."* If the task of a mental revolution looks or sounds too difficult then the saying from Margaret Mead should encourage Africans. It does not have to be drastic; but the change needs to take place and a few committed Africans and their leaders can make it a reality. No one says change will be easy. This is because many African heads of states would not like to give up their power and influence, but like a friend of mine said, "I will rather have one percent of a multi-million dollar business than a hundred percent of nothing". African leaders would need to give up something for the general good. The people too should be willing to put all hands on deck and work for an Africa they can be proud of anywhere, anytime.

The starting point would be to reinforce the ties between the existing regional bodies. The Regional Economic Commissions (RECs) should become each other's keeper by looking at the similarities between the countries, their comparative advantages, work together to make the regions stronger and more economically viable then gradually move to all of Africa.

If Africa means anything to Africans, one sign of unity will be great pomp in the celebration of *Africa day* (May 25, as declared by the founding fathers) in all African countries. This needs to be done in such pomp and style and media coverage that no event ever surpasses it. It should be an annual holyday, a day on which all come out as one Africa, to prove their unity and strength.

Evidence from different sources shows that Africa is the poorest continent in the universe in terms of development, but not in terms of natural resources because the continent is blessed with an abundance of natural resources for which there is a market. However, Africa has been unable to add value to the resources before exporting and that is why it gains very little on its natural resources. Africa would need to make an inventory of what it has and orient some of its educational system towards the cultivation and transformation of its resources in order to achieve maximum benefit from them.

Africa does not have to reinvent the wheel because most of the work has been done by the other continents. All it needs to do is to look at best practices from other countries, improve on them and implement those practices. Therefore the road to development for Africa should not be as tedious as it was for the other countries and continents.

For Africa to be truly developed, its communication, road and infrastructure network has to become a priority. Africa needs to sit and identify its trans-Africa road network, communication network and electrical possibilities and start working on them collectively.

The cultural values, ethics, arts and morals that Africa has lost through migration and colonization and assimilation should be strongly revived and shared across the continent. *Africa day* would be a good day to showcase all these lost values and competitions with huge prizes can be organized by the African Union at the continental level.

Donors bring aid in different forms to Africa. Foreign Direct investments through fair trade can contribute to Africa's development; however the aid scenario needs to be revisited. The billions of dollars in aid which is said to have been spent in Africa may be real but that is just an indirect way in which the donor countries simply give with the left hand and take back the money with the right hand through administrative costs and expatriate salaries. Africa needs to re-evaluate the scenario in order to decide if it wants to continue accepting the status quo from the donors.

The bottom line is that if Africa wants to develop, it cannot do so in its present fragmented and inefficient state. Africa would have to forget idiosyncratic boundaries imposed on it by colonial masters who did not take into consideration any socio-cultural affiliations when the boundaries were put. A mental revolution has to take place and the time is now for that revolution to take place. Africa and Africans are ready to move forward, the question is, are they willing to take the challenge or lose another opportunity to propel the continent to development?

Lament for my Land
I cry for the pupil who knows that he has to give his lunch to the bus driver in order to get a good seat on the bus.
I cry for the pupil who needs to take a packet of sugar to school to get good marks.

I cry for the youth who has left secondary school and can speak neither the Queen's language nor Napoleon's.
I cry for the youth who wants to work but has no marketable skills.
I cry for the University graduate who writes *concours* after *concours* and never makes it through the orals
I cry for the graduate who goes around with torn jeans and a defeated look.
I cry for the graduates who ten years after leaving University can no longer enter the public service because he is 33.
I cry for the graduate who has to change his age over and over but retires never having worked.
I cry for the graduate who sleeps forever because he could no longer move his feet.
I cry for the man who has to retire at 55 just when he became a master of his craft.
I cry for the man who has to compile papers to have his dues
I cry for the man who paid for land which was sold to four other people.
I cry for the man who took years for his case to be heard in court.
I cry for the one who died before his verdict came out.

I cry for the woman who died in child birth because there was no hospital or doctor in the village.
I cry for the baby who survived alone while the money meant for the hospital went into another's pocket.
I cry for the child who wants to go to school but cannot because there is no school.
I cry for the woman in the village who has nothing to eat while the money that could have brought her water is used to settle political issues.
I weep for the parliamentarian who swears to represent his people but ends up blackmailing the system to send him on missions he doesn't go.
I cry for my country, the land of milk and honey where some have too much and others nothing.
I cry for Africa because I don't know where to turn.

Being African
Being African has nothing to do with the colour of my skin.
It has nothing to do with the texture or colour of my eyes.
Being African has nothing to do with how straight or kinky my hair is.
Being African has nothing to do with the language I speak or the ones that I don't speak.
It has got nothing even with the continent I come from or where it is found on the world map.
Being African starts with the music in my ears, the blood pulsating through my veins.
The uniqueness and shape of my body,
The smell of earth on rainy days,
The sound of animals far off,
The height of the trees, and the lushness of the grass,
The brownness of the earth and the sands for miles on end,
The blue sea and the blue sky.
Being African is the greeting on the road from a total stranger;
The uncles and aunts who are not related to me;

The smile from a neighbour and the blessings from a toothless
old woman;
The knock at the door at any time and the assurance that the
door will be opened and I will be welcomed.
Being African is the laughter I hear from the villagers as they
drink palm wine under the trees near huts that are thatched.
Being African is the smell of flowers that grow in the wild;
The fresh vegetables from the farm, and the fowls that walk
round the house.
The dawn that is signalled by the crow of the cock;
The whisper of the trees as the wind blows their leaves.
Being African is the heat, the joy of sharing and the bonds
between us.
Being African is the culture I grew up with.
Being African is the way of life I know and accept.

Development, the Whiteman's way has eroded the
values I hold dear, the Africa I knew. It is changing, the
landscape of the Africa I knew. I wonder this development;
whose development is it? Will this development lead to
happiness? What is happiness? If there was a thermometer to
measure happiness I wonder what the results would be. The
couple living a simple life in the village in a one room,
thatched, mud house, with no amenities or "modern facilities"
is healthier and happier than the couple riding a Mercedes
Benz in the city. The African is happier than the rest of the
world.

When I completed my MBA in the States, I did an
analysis of a case study concerning Hewlett Packard. After I
sent them a copy of the report as a courtesy, I was called from
their headquarters in Texas and offered a job. I could not
accept the job as I explained to them, I was a married African
woman and I had to return to join my husband. What does
your husband do? I told them he was a Translator Interpreter
who had studied in George Town University. So let him come
too, we can give him a job. Without asking my husband or

missing a heartbeat, I answered that as an African, a woman goes where the husband is and not the other way around. The man sighed and thanked me for the report. I returned home and it took me a year to get a job.

There is a lot that is good and a lot that is bad in being African. Nevertheless, as a proud African, I think that the good outweighs the bad and that we have a lot to cherish in our fatherland; the land of our ancestors, this land where the Son of GOD walked. Sometimes when I use an HP computer, I wonder what my life would have been like had I taken the job with HP and moved my family to the USA. I would have missed the family who gave my baby and I baths when I gave birth, or missed the warmth and tender loving care of the family, all the house help I had and the fact that my children could grow up and call even people who are not related to them, auntie and uncle. I would have missed the dust, the rain and the sunshine and the special smell of rain falling on the ground, the family members who just popped in unannounced and expected a meal and a bed and a smile to go with all of that and at the end of their stay expect you to pay their fare back home.

References

1. Collier, Paul:2007 The Bottom Billion
2. Ibid
3. Dollar, David and William Easterly. The search for the Key: Aid, Investment, and Policies in Africa.
4. Ibid
5. Ivan Hoffman
6. Mr. Cheick Sidi Diarra: Under-Secretary-General, Special Adviser on Africa and High Representative for the Least Developed Countries, Landlocked Developing Countries and Small Island Developing States on "Trade and Development for Africa's Prosperity: Action and Direction" during the high-level segment UNCTAD XII Conference, Accra, Ghana, 21 April 2008
7. Wikipedia. http://en.wikipedia.org/wiki/Colonisation_of_Africa
8. Ibid. http://en.wikipedia.org/wiki/Colonisation_of_Africa
9. Ibid. http://en.wikipedia.org/wiki/Colonisation_of_Africa
10. Ibid. http://en.wikipedia.org/wiki/Colonisation_of_Africa
11. Ibid. http://en.wikipedia.org/wiki/Colonisation_of_Africa
12. Ibid. http://en.wikipedia.org/wiki/Colonisation_of_Africa
13. Melissa Snell
14. Wikipedia. http://en.wikipedia.org/wiki/Colonisation_of_Africa
15. Ibid. http://en.wikipedia.org/wiki/Colonisation_of_Africa
16. Ibid. http://en.wikipedia.org/wiki/Colonisation_of_Africa
17. Nelly Nyagah *Getting it right with joint ventures TradeInvestAfrica*

Bibliography

1. Collier, Paul. (2007). *The Bottom Billion*: *Why the Poorest Countries are failing and what can be done About It.* Oxford and New York: Oxford University Press.

2. World Bank. (2010). World Development Indicators.

3. Easterly, William (2007). *The White Man's Burden.* Oxford University Press

4. World Health Organization

5. Moyo, Dambisa. *Dead Aid.* Why aid is not working and how there is a better way for Africa.

6. Dollar, David and William Easterly. *The search for the Key: Aid, Investment, and Policies in Africa*

7. Snell, Melissa. "Splendor in Medieval Africa a visit to Mali's medieval past". *About.com Guide*

8. Moghalu, Kingsley. Strategic approach to foreign direct investment in Nigeria. Keynote speech presented at the Business and investment forum for Nigeria held in Zurich January 20-22, 2009.

9. Speeches: UNCTAD XII Conference, Accra, Ghana, 21 April 2008

10. UNCTAD web site

11. African Union web site

12. Wikipedia web site: The free dictionary.

13. NIV Bible

Beatrice Fri Bime

14.   Hoffman, Ivan. *Respect for laws*. http://www.ivanhoffman.com/respect.html

15. Nyagah, Nelly. Getting it right with joint ventures. *TradeInvestAfrica Tue, 10 Aug 2010*

16. "Women in Parliaments: World Classification". Inter-Parliamentary Union. May 14, 2012.

17. Aiden Southall: "State formations in Africa"

18. Kah Walla: 'Whose Daughters are we?' Talk at American Embassy, Yaoundé, 2012.

19. Shundzev: A Nso cultural and intellectual forum

About the Author

Beatrice Fri Bime was born in the Bamenda highlands in Cameroon. She is a consultant and has worked in various capacities with the government, the United Nations, and international NGOs. After primary and secondary education in Cameroon she moved to the USA where she obtained an MBA from the University of Wisconsin-Whitewater.

She runs a foundation which enables young people get the kind of education she advocates. Fri Bime is the Author of two previous books *Mystique: a collection of lake myths* and *Someplace, Somewhere.* She has also published some poems in the US and Cameroon. She enjoys cooking, entertaining and dancing.

Beatrice Fri Bime